That Thou Art

That Thou Art

The Unknown Dimensions

Indu Pande

MOTILAL BANARSIDASS INTERNATIONAL
DELHI

First Edition : Delhi, 2026

© Author
All Rights Reserved

ISBN : 978-93-47683-06-0

Also available at :

MOTILAL BANARSIDASS INTERNATIONAL

41 U.A. Bungalow Road, (Back Lane) Jawahar Nagar, Delhi-110007
4261/3 (Basement), Ansari Road, Darya Ganj, New Delhi-110002
Shop#. 6, 241, Luz Ginza Complex, Luz Corner, Mylapore, Chennai - 600004
12/1A, 2nd Floor, Bankim Chatterjee Street, Kolkata - 700073

Stockist : Motilal Books, Ashok Rajpath, Near Kali Mandir, Patna-800004

No part of this book may be reproduced in any form or by any
electronic or mechanical means including information storage
and retrieval systems without permission in writing from the
publishers, except by a reviewer who may quote brief
passages in a review.

Printed in India by
MOTILAL BANARSIDASS INTERNATIONAL

Preface

The book is a philosophical novel set against the backdrop of Indian spiritual traditions, exploring the intersection of ancient wisdom and modern psychology and scientific thought through a tapestry of dialogue, inner search, and cross cultural understanding.

The story follows the central character of the book, Anna Lindermier's journey to India, to familiarize herself with the elements of contemplative psychology as elaborated in the old Indian texts relating to Yoga and Vedanta.

The book is a work of reflective fiction that explores the meeting ground of psychology, culture and inner experience.

Through the journey of it's central character, it examines enduring questions about human nature, violence and compassion, reason intellect and intuitive wisdom, and search for meaning in a fast changing world.

Anna's spiritual and intellectual journey leads her from the structured world of western psychology and psycho analysis to the deeply symbolic terrain of Indian philosophy, which also reflects the fundamental elements of Indian psychology, which is being researched upon in recent times. She travels to India to seek a direct insight into the Yogic and Vedantic traditions.

Set across contemporary India- from forest and wild life reserves to villages, rivers and ashrams- the narrative brings the Western analytical thought into dialogue with the Eastern contemplative traditions. Without idealising either of the two, it presents culture as a living and evolving process shaped by history, belief and experience.

Nature, memory and myth play a vital role in the story, offering symbolic and psychological depth. The forest, the tiger, the mountain and the river serve not only as settings for the story, but also are metaphors for instinct, transformation and self inquiry.

Rather than delivering dry exposition, the novel attempts to weave Vedanta and Yoga philosophy into a series of vibrant discourses and storytelling. It explores various schools of thought including Buddhism, Charvak materialism , non dual Advaita school of Vedanta, while addressing the modern misappropriation, commercialisation, and commodification of spiritual concepts, thereby diluting it's rich content.

This is not a book of conclusions, but of exploration. It invites the readers to reflect, to question the inherited assumptions and to consider perspectives that lie beyond the conventional boundaries of thought.

The attempt is to foster among the readers an interest in psychology, philosophy and cross cultural understanding by offering a contemplative journey into what it means to be human.

This book grew out of questions rather than answers, and many people- knowingly and unknowingly became part of that questioning.

I am grateful to all those people who crossed my path during the writing of this book through conversation, silence or disagreement.

My gratitude to my wife, children and family who stood by me during the writing of the book as well as friends and well wishers .

I acknowledge the landscapes that shaped this work- mountains, forests, rivers and streams that offered both solitude and perspective.

I am thankful for all the wisdom traditions- Eastern and Western- that informed my thinking.

I am grateful to Ms. Manisha Pant and Dr. Sunita Pant Bansalfor their support and guidance. I express my gratitude to M/s. Motilal Banarasidass International, who have finally brought the book into light.

Content

Chapter - 1

ANNA

"Aahana", the first golden rays of the sun lighting the earth and energizing it had descended at dawn and had managed to sneak through a slight opening between the curtains on the window and were gently caressing her eyelids. She was in a deep slumber oblivious of the world around her with all its concomitant worries, stress and tension. Knocking at your inbox -no bills to be paid, no money to be recovered, no creditors. Habitually an early riser, it was perhaps the jet lag of Munich Delhi flight coupled with fatigue of the Delhi Ramnagar road journey, which needed to be compensated by a few extra hours of sleep. Moreover, neither the road nor the traffic was very friendly with road jams and frequent diversions on undulating dirt roads through the countryside, which did not present a very pleasant landscape.

She had checked in at "Aahna" resort yesterday on her India trip which was to commence with a visit to the internationally acclaimed Corbett National Park. The park- a tiger conservation reserve was named after a local hunter conservationist Edward James Corbett popularly known as Jim Corbett. The local villagers in this North West Central Himalayan region of earlier generations held him in great regard. Corbett the legend had been a cult figure among the local village folk because he had been instrumental in getting rid of many man-eating tigers and leopards and big cats gone astray, and showing allegedly deviant behavior due to either an injury or disability resulting in difficulty in hunting its prey in the wild. Having found humans as an easy prey, and having tasted human blood became a menace. The story she was told started with the man eater of Champawat, believed to have killed more than four hundred persons.

Anna Lindermier, was the daughter of Dr. Franz Lindermier, a psycho therapist and Bertina Lindermier, a clinical psychologist, thereby had psychology in her genes. The visit to the park was not in her original itinerary. What motivated her visit to India was to familiarize her with the elements of contemplative psychology, professed by the ancient sage psychologists of India – a mystical novelty from a western psychologist's point of view. However a casual reference of 'Project Tiger' by her travel agent touched a rather sensitive chord in her psyche. It had bought back memories of the tragic Nanda Devi expedition of 1976. The story was told to her by Benedikt Berg, her mountaineer boyfriend. Nanda Devi Unsoeld had worked with Project Tiger in Nepal.Willy Unsoeld an accomplished American mountaineer and Everester, was so mesmerized by the beauty of Nanda Devi mountain peaks in Indian Himalayas decided to name his daughter Nanda Devi. She had in 1974 decided to climb the mountain after which she had been named. She was part of the joint Indo-American Nanda Devi expedition of 1976. What was envisaged as "a Family based pilgrimage to a holy place", ended in a tragedy when Devi at the age of twenty two got ill in one of the advanced camps, refused to be rescued and her remains were consigned to the snows.

Munich the city where Anna was born and brought up was to play host to the Olympic Games. As growing child she was told of the forthcoming event as a symbol of healthy competition, among people from all parts of the globe. In a sporting event like this, each participant apart from trying to excel the others also made an attempt to excel his own self. All the reserves of energy and strength, physical mental were to be brought forth. The playground offered the opportunity to each sports person irrespective of his class, caste, creed, race or religion to realize his or her own potential to play, compete, excel and win. The victory was to be followed by the presentation of medals, gold silver and bronze in recognition of a person or team having proved better than the other in the fairest possible manner.

The Olympic village in Munich in August 1972 thronged with thousands of athletes, sports persons their coaches' managers etc. representing their nations from all over the globe. All of them full of optimism were enthusiastic to prove their mettle and outshine others with dreams of medals galore. 'Die Heiteren Spiele'- the cheerful games was the prevalent spirit. Olympic Games had come to Germany after a gap of thirty six years following the Berlin games of the Nazi era.

Here was New Germany, keen to offer a contrast to the happenings of the Nazi era. However, unfortunately on the fateful morning of 5th September 1972, a group of Palestinian disguised as athletes, using stolen keys entered the quarters of the Israeli Olympic team, shot two of members and took nine hostages. The hostages were also subsequently killed. The rescue operation by the German police who were perhaps not sufficiently trained or equipped for such an operation failed and the final outcomes was a cryptic announcement. "They are all gone". Young Anna not yet fully emerged from her childhood all this while excited about the Olympics asked her mother innocently as to who they were and where have they all gone?

Those who departed were innocent people said Bertina to her daughter and those responsible for their departure were also humans. They were the people whose human values had been overtaken by animal instincts. In certain ways they behaved worse than the animals. In the animals world there are no senseless killings. It is the old evolutionary principle of survival of the fittest along with struggle for existence. An animal killed the other for his survival or defense. A predator kills its prey when hungry. The honey bees sting the stealer to protect their produce which ultimately leads to their own death. It is the tragedy of the so called civilized humans that we always find an excuse for our own nefarious activities. Even the most dastardly act of killing innocent people is often justified on one ground or other. Wars are justified on the patriotic principle of nationalism. A person or a member of a militant group treated a terrorist by the outside world is considered as a potential martyr in his own group, eulogized for fighting for an ideal or objective, often a political one. The violent behavior is often justified on grounds of a perceived injustice to the individual or the social group, and what prevails is the distorted interpretation of the idea of retributive justice. It is the same psychology, where the narrow self interest of nations veiled with the ideal of sovereignty leads to war among the civilized nations. The child in her found it hard to come to terms with the tragedy. How could humans, the so called evolved torch bearers of civilization could stoop to a level where in their ego dominated behavior, they think of eliminating their fellow beings. Something must have gone wrong with their psyche, which needs to be undone. Perhaps the foundation was already laid for her career as a psycho-therapist.

Anna, the growing child often dreamt of masked men holding sten guns, about to fire on innocent revelers in a carnival during the Christmas time. All attempts to scare them with a shriek always failed till one day the shriek became a high pitched thunder like angry growl of a tiger and they all disappeared, dropping their guns behind. Cowards all of them, she concluded. When she woke up, she shared the dream with her mother.

Bertina realizing that the Munich massacre had traumatized the child, gently explained to her that life is full of experiences, sweet sour and indifferent. We all have to devise our own coping mechanisms and strategies and nothing should permanently scare us. Life was all about leaving the unpleasant past behind, learning its lessons and looking forward with optimism to the future. Bertina as a clinical psychologist was well trained in psychological principles and methods. It was a minor issue, but for the fact that her own daughter was involved. Anna had to be reassured, and her self confidence restored. The nightmares gradually disappeared and Anna moved forward leaving the past behind.

After having completed a programme on psychiatry from the University of Heidelberg, Anna went to Zurich to the 'Jung Institute of Analytical Psychology' for a training programme. She had finally joined as a faculty member at the Ludwig Maximilian University of Munich, an institution with more than five hundred years old tradition. There she learnt about George Sieber, alumni of LMU, the police psychologist, who had been rather prescient about a commando attack on Israelis in Munich, and was summarily removed after the massacre in a cover up like operation. He had predicted twenty six worst case scenarios of which the twenty first imagined scenario had actualized. Did he have a dream earlier? Were dreams prescient about future events as was belief in the Pre-Freudian era. The incident for her had left many questions unanswered besides initially strengthening her resolve to pursue a career in psychotherapy.

She often wondered about the hyper competitive aspect of human nature like some of their simian ancestors, baboons and some chimpanzees that were rather aggressive in their behavior leading to conflict and violence. Perhaps there was a yet unidentified violent gene in the humans which nurtured by human intelligence gets wrongly oriented to devise means of aggression.

The militant always justified his violent action either by playing the exploited victim card, claiming justice, or by placing himself on high moral grounds, identifying himself with an ideal created by a myth. He then identified himself with it voluntarily or by indoctrination.

No wonder that Jung remarked that after nearly two thousand years of Christian history, instead of Paradise and life everlasting, we have had world war of Christian nations with barbed wire entanglements and poisonous gases- what a debacle in heaven and earth. The weaponry has changed over the years, but strife continues unabated she thought. The swords spears and shields were donning the walls of museums as artifacts, had been replaced by deadlier nuclear bombs, assault rifles, missiles with nuclear heads, and weapons of mass destruction. Victor was always right, the vanquished the villain. The soldier killing his enemy on the battle field is as innocent as the victim he kills. No wonder it has been said by some philosophers that the defenselessness of the potential victim tempts the tormentor, the angelic confidence of the child who has no refuge or appeal that sets the vile blood on fire.

Who was right? Hobbes who held the view that we are 'Born savages', only making compromise by way of diluting our selfishness and savagery to the extent that we could survive in a society, or Rousseau who maintained that we were 'Born free' only to be corrupted by the environment. Is ours essential nature human or brutal.? Is the world we live in ugly, evil, depressing full of strife and conflict or there is light at the end of the tunnel? These are the vexed questions of life where scientist, philosophers, psychologists, sociologists, historians, and anthropologist have to provide answers.

It depends as to what appeals to a person as an individual. That's why some of the philosophers have held a view that life is a 'Mysterium Tremendum', which keeps us hoping and living. Even under the most adverse circumstances we always approach the future with optimism. Tomorrow is another day, bound to be better than today.

It was Hegel chastised, realizing that spirit of the age was weary of too much change wrote than after forty years of war and immeasurable confusion, an old heart might rejoice to see an end to it all, and the beginning of a period of peaceful satisfaction. Even a philosopher of strife and antinomies, proponent of dialectic of growth also had a right at the age of sixty to ask for peace. It is said that old people delve in the past, young one looking to the future and rest of them struggling to cope up with the present. She was still young and imbued with a optimism which she was confident would never fade.

It has been held by the historians of philosophy that Germany's great age ended with Goethe, Hegel, and Beethoven, and Schopenhauer was there to 'force' philosophy to face the raw reality of life'. Schopenhauer sensing a chaotic universe pessimistic in his approach 'opened the eyes of the psychologists to the subtle depth of an omnipresent force of instinct'. His idea of will to live in which everything was rooted was the main cause of struggle suffering and pain- the great evil which accounted for the misery of all beings. In his scheme of things will prevented our reason intellect and consciousness.

It was in the winters once in a while, Anna could see the silhouette of snow capped peaks of Bavarian pre-alps. She was keen to respond to the mountains call and as it happened that at a friend's party she met Benedikt Berg, an adventure seeker and travel Writer working for REISELUST. As his name implied he was born for the mountains. It started with some simple easy treks in Mitten Wald and then some training in Peter Habeler's ski and mountaineering school in Mayrhofen, then slightly more difficult treks in the

Bavarian Alps and then a few courses in Chamonix and then Mont Blanc and Matter horn. Inspired by Hermann Buhl, who had tried the Alpine way of climbing the mountains in Himalayas, he was fortunate to have landed in Chamoli district of India in the central Himalayas to do a story on Nanda Devi. However to his consternation he realized that the expeditions to Nanda Devi summit had been prohibited because a large number of mountaineering expeditions had led to damage the ecology of the area. However, he went up to the Laata village. The majestic beauty of the area made him realize Willy Unsoeld,s fascination for the peaks, who subsequently had named his daughter as Devi.

Devi was a member of the tragic Nanda Devi expectation of 1976, lost her life and her mortal remains consigned to the snows of the Himalayas, below the summit. The elders of the village recounted that the porters thought that Devi was divinity itself, who had come back to her abode, the 'Goddess of Joy'. However, mountaineering experts thought otherwise According to them there was nothing spiritual or divine about it. It was a human tragedy, plain and simple, due to certain mistakes and lack of coordination.

The Indian denizens of these remote mountain regions considered the Himalayas as the abode of the gods and that's why worshipped the mountains.

The general message was that the mountains were sacred and had to be approached with respect and reverence. Himalayas, was also the abode of Lord Shiva in his earthly frame and also his father in law in an anthropomorphic mode. For Benedikt all this while mountains were mountains and humans were humans. This kind of relationship between insentient nature and sentient humans was something strange for him. Is there some magic in these mountains, which goes beyond our normal understanding? Is it the geography of an area where you are perilously perched at the base of an unstable mountain prone to landslide, avalanches, which conditions your thought in a manner that your belief in forces unseen, super natural so as to say gets strengthened. Since the Himalayan bug had already bitten him, he decided to visit glaciers in the Bhagirathi valley the source of the sacred Ganges. He had heard about Shivling peak, the Indian Matterhorn, from a fellow climber in Mayrhofen, and finally crossing the Gomukh glacier, with its rocks, morraine and frozen ice, landed at Tapovan, base camp for climbers in that region. There was the Nehru Institute of Mountaineering (NIM) close by which trained people in this region. On his way back at Gangotri, where a temple dedicated to Goddess Ganga was situated he decided to halt for a night. By now he had been suitably impressed by the aura and majesty of Himalayas and internally committed to himself to visit the area more often. On way back he visited Tripatha Ashram at Harshil.

Chapter - 2

AAHNA

After having checked in at the resort, in her five days itinerary she tentatively had kept the next day for rest, recreation and leisure and participation in wellness programmes offered by the resort, which included yoga, spa, Ayurvedic massage, swimming and nature walk. Two days for wildlife and rest she left undecided to be chalked out later. Today, there was no urgency for a safari in the wildlife park, so she decided to join the yoga session in the morning.Coming out of the hall she met a young lady who greeted her with a smile and introduced herself as a member of the "Aahna family".

"How long have you been in this resort and what has the experience been like" queried the young lady. I checked in only yesterday evening was quite tired, the journey fatigue and after an early dinner crashed on to the bed. Got up late this morning and perhaps the yoga session was my first exposure to the place and I found it interesting, said Anna. Our motto is 'Atithi Devo Bhava', a guest is to be revered as a god, a line taken from a Vedic Scripture called Taittiriya Upanishad. 'Atithi' is as uninvited guest where tithi or the date is not specified as different from an "Abhyagata' who is an invited guest, who stands somewhat lower in the hierarchy. So a total stranger is more than welcome and our endeavour is to provide a wholesome experience which would include ecotourism, leisure, wellness and a window to the local culture.

"That sounds interesting", said Anna. However, how come you preferred Scottish bagpipe to welcome the guests instead of local musical instrument. We in India have a great assimilative capacity when it comes to culture. We adopt, and assimilate the elements of alien culture which we like. It was the case with Scottish bag pipe converted into a 'Mashak Been', a localized version of Bag pipe, which reached India through the British Army. The foot soldiers, mostly Indians took it home and tuned it to their folk songs and music. We try to provide a local flavor in every experience including the food we serve without compromising on the quality or taste.

We consider ourselves fortunate being located in this Central Himalayan region, where nature has been very liberal in bestowing its bounty in terms of snow capped mountains, meandering rivers, verdant valleys, forests with extensive bio-diversity, almost everything except for the sea. In India all creation is credited to a cosmic scarifice by the creator. The law of sacrifice rules supreme in ancient philosophy and mythology. No wonder the sea of Tethys located here sacrificed itself as the progenitor of the mountains and got buried somewhere deep in the womb of mother earth. Because of abundant resources which the nature provides in this region, in mythology it has been said that the treasure of Kubera- Lord of Wealth is located somewhere in Alka puri, the mountains in the North Eastern part of the region. The young lady from the 'Aahna Family' suggested that they carry on the conversation to the breakfast table.

While the spread for the breakfast was reflective of local flavor, with various regional recipes it also was a window to the cultural transformation that new India was undergoing. It was now the era of multi cuisine restaurants. Chinese, Thai had become passe.

Vietnamese, Korean Mexican, Italian, Mediterranean were the in thing. The change in epicurean preferences is denotive of a style statement. So perhaps had been the case with people visiting the National park. While some of them may have had genuine interest in wildlife, forests and bio-diversity, for most of the visitors it was more of a fashionable style statement. To be environmentally conscious and talk of conservation and sustainability had been fashionable. India, predominantly still rural, reflected in cultural terms a strange pattern cum paradox of quasi consumerism,conservatism, and an ongoing struggle between modernity and tradition.

While on the one hand nature was still worshipped inform of deities, sun, moon, fire, and over arching gods forming the orthodox trinity of Brahma, Vishnu, Mahesh, creator sustainer and destroyer which subsumed and replaced many of the Vedic gods, and local deities, it at the same time aspired to be modern, utilitarian and had been bitten by bug of consumerism. A quasi consumer society which revered nature and yet was willing to commodify it for economic advantage.

The conversation at the breakfast table now was about the essential elements of culture and Indian tradition. Culture by itself is somewhat of a nebulous concept which can be interpreted in different ways.

It is culture which differentiates the human from the animal. An evolutionary biologist or a psychologist may think otherwise. Maybe the difference lies in the size of brain, development of mind, intellect and the nature of consciousness - yet another area of nebulous intricacy.

The resort was a place where one got a sanitized version of culture. It was frequented mostly by a section of the society, who apparently symbolized a transition to modern from traditional in the sense that a visit to wildlife park and seeing a tiger in the wild was enough material to be discussed in the drawing rooms of Metropolitan cities over a glass of wine preferably from South Africa, Argentina or New Zealand because French and Italian wines had become obsolete. It was too early to firm up her ideas about Indian Culture except that it had to be viewed in the context of a social tradition undergoing periodic changes and a prevalent undercurrent of an assumed religiosity rather than spirituality.

Does India of the old survive anywhere except in a few shrinking hermitages called Ashrams and libraries and maybe few academic institutions. Anna realized that it was the wrong place to find the answers. It was not an 'ascetic retreat' for meditation. It was for a 'pleasurable experience' which could bolster a person's ego to claim that they have been able to get a 'unique experience' while visiting a much touted National Park.

Anna was a person of internet age from west working in an institution, which ipso facto meant that she had gathered many facts about India before visiting it and had taken lessons in Hindi. Since contemplative psychology was her area of interest, so philosophy which was linked to psychology in India and religion culture and civilization adjuncts were very much part of it, were therefore reflected in the mythology, Epics and folklore.

The discussion again reverted to yoga and wellness therapy.

Anna felt that yoga in its totality with its spiritual connotations was perhaps a very strong symbol of the Indian culture. However, the Indian civilizational and cultural story is not very simple. Any explanation or analysis which ignores the Vedic civilization and its remnants is inadequate, to say the least. Major discussion on philosophy related aspects she would postpone for Tripatha Ashram which was going to be her final destination during this visit.

They decided to meet before lunch to carry on the discussion from where they had left it

When they met before lunch, she was offered a beer which she promptly refused. I thought Germany was a beer country said the Aahna lady. Well certainly replied Anna but 'Nicht Sein Beer.' The beer you get here perhaps is not my Beer. Is Lowenbrau available in your bar? "No sorry, we have Budweiser, Carlsberg Fosters, King Fisher replied the lady." I am too much of a Bavarian who still supports the 'Reinheitsgebot' and resist any attempt to change it. What's that supposed to be? asked the lady. It is the time honoured German purity of Beer Law, wherein German Beer initially could have only limited ingredients.

Hops, Barley and water while subsequently yeast, coriander and Bay leaf were permitted.

It is part of our culinary cultural tradition and I am proud of it. The sense of purity is embedded in the German Psyche. "Was it not that this sense of racial purity distorted to an extent that a whole lot of innocents were massacred during the Nazi era". Yes it is a stigma with which we been living with and continue to remain. Violence can never be justified in a civilized society. Civilization then tends to loose its meaning and significance.

What would you then prefer for a drink, perhaps a wine? Hope you don't have a 'Reheitsgebot' like law for Wines, asked the lady. We have German Wine Law of 1971, which is yet to become part of a tradition. It classifies wines according to 'Must Weight', a measure of amount of sugar in a grape juice. It is not embedded in our psyche the way Beer Law is. Beer Law is a kind of National Symbol, especially for a Bavarian like me, said Anna.

"We have had endless discussions with my mountaineer boyfriend Benedict Berg, who always found the German law archaic which needs to be scrapped sooner than later, yet continues to be part of a minority group of German Beer drinkers. However, the law does not apply to foreign manufactures, 'What was the rational for such a law?' Perhaps at that time the idea must have been to prevent unscrupulous brewers from adding toxic substance and adulterating the product with something which could make it a health hazard.

In German Psyche there is a love for order, yet there is an attraction to everything unfathomable which does not easily fit into categories.

This strange contradiction is perhaps inherent in the human psyche. In some societies it remains hidden clouded by materialistic doctrines while in some societies like India it is reflected in a strong religiosity. Hegel the philosopher, a symbol of Germany's greatest age after having graduated from Tubingen had to earn his bread by tutoring in Berne and Frankfort. After his father's death he inherited a princely sum of $ 1500, and gave up tutoring and wrote to his friend Schelling seeking advice as to where to settle. His preference for a place which he would like to stay should be one where simple food and abundant books should be available along with 'eine gutes bier'. So whether it be the great philosopher or a railroad worker, 'Bier' was very much part of the German life style.

It was time for lunch, and out on a holiday Anna thought she could afford the luxury of an afternoon siesta. The doctors these days say that an afternoon siesta even twice a week keeps the heart healthy.

All of us in the vicinity of the Park have as a marketing strategy taken advantage of the 'Brand Equity' of the name 'Corbett'.

However, she was a little blunt in asking Anna as to what kindled her interest in Yoga and contemplative psychology which motivated her enough to undertake her Indian journey. She had as she said earlier, access to most of the texts on the internet. 'Loss of originality' was the prompt reply, not from the point of view of idea or thought, but language. A Sanskrit word I was told has different meaning in different context. I came here to a find out a person, a Guru who could explain the context and the right meaning and interpretation. It all started at Jung Institute of Analytical Psychology in

Zurich, where a fellow participant in a programme introduced her to Hauer,s views on 'Der Yoga im Lichte der Psychotherapy' and Keyserling's much acclaimed. 'The Travel Diary of a philosopher', wherein it was stated that the new psychology was a rediscovery of what was already known by the ancient seer sages of India. It referred to old Indian 'science of the soul'. Hauer and Keyserling led to Jung. "Ein Indisher Weg Zurer Selbst"-an Indian way to self- Now it was getting curiouser. Jung was being brutally frank when he confessed that the meaning of yoga for India, he could not comment on because of lack of experience. However for the west with the prevalent psychic anarchy, culture specific methods of psychological discipline were likely to lead to 'mimetic madness'. Kundalini Yoga in psychological terms was an introversion process likely to induce personality changes and a method of 'psychic hygiene' was likely to lead to 'mimetic madness' in Europe and had to be suitably modified. West will have to produce its own yoga in course of time to in consonance with the principles of Christianity. Founding father of Analytical psychology was impressed to the extent that he thought of devising what he thought of as a religious and philosophic practice in an altogether new format- a new recipe suited to the European palate. At the same time, there were critics in Germany, who thought of Yoga and Tantrism as a psycho-spiritual science fiction and 'sexual acrobatics that could put to shame even the most imaginative of pornographer.' I consider myself to be born in the internet era so as to have access to the multifarious narratives regarding any subject, a luxury to which the likes of Freud, Jung and Adler didn't have access to.

Had it been otherwise the dimensions of Freud,s id, ego and super ego would have been much larger. Though it is not very fair to generalize, yet I think that the ancient Indians as different from the modern one had realized the inadequacy of empirical experience, which lead to desire to know what was beyond the normal sensory or mental spectrum, and explore the unknown dimensions.

In order to appear scientific and rational, perhaps the psychologists of the Freudian era, his disciples Adler and Jung were baulked down by the philosophy of scientific positivism. The very idea of the unconscious, the large submerged part of the iceberg that was mind itself was revolutionary to which they subsequently contributed in a significant manner. Analyzing, adding, subtracting, deleting, according to their own ideas yet within the bounds of so called rationality and intellect. None of them thought about a faculty superior to intellect, the intuitive experience which prima facie appeared to be unscientific. It was limited to body and mind, the psychosomatic equations, whereas the ancients had introduced the third element of spirituality, whose validity was seriously questioned in the west because it delved beyond the empirical domain. Plato who had talked of soul and universals has already been diluted to large extent in Europe with the emergence of scientific evolutionary thought where God becomes a delusion, so perhaps spirit does not stand as of date much of a chance. However, I thought that India being the birthplace of contemplative psychology where the ontological base and epistemological super structure are in harmony, I might be able to find some learned knowledgeable person, a Guru in the local parlance who may be able to enlighten me. One who can fill up the gap between critical reason and supra rational intuition.

What better place than the abode of gods? Well the visit to the park was only incidental, but hope it adds value to my visit. Anna had realized that just three days in India and the bon homie here had resulted in a penetration of certain Indianness in her subconscious.

Taking their cue from Darwin, Haeckel and their followers the scientific optimist felt that neurons, synapses neuro transmitter etc., the integral neural systems coupled with the discovery of elusive Higgs Boson some day in future will be able to provide all the explanations. Well there is this interesting story which Adler parting ways with Freud liked to tell. Three children were taken to the zoo for the first time. As they stood before the lion's cage, one of them shrank behind his mothers skirts and said "I want to go home". The second child stood where he was, very pale and trembling and said, "I am not a bit frightened". The third glared at lion fiercely and asked his mother "Shall I spit at it?" The three children really felt inferior, but each expressed his feelings in his own way, consonant with his style of life. Sense of inferiority led people strive to gain superiority and "mastery of the external world". Adler's earlier choice as a physician was driven by the idea "to overcome death and fear of death."

Now I don't really know whether being human ipso facto leads to sense of inferiority and generated epistemic curiosity. Idea of being ignorant about most of the things and birth life and death in particular, lead to my interest in contemplative psychology, going far beyond the boundaries of modern Para psychology and trans-personal psychology.

Does the elusive 'Turiya'- the transcendent fourth exist or was it confined to the fanciful imagination of the ancient seer sages of India? Can I find definite answers or in any case if I am able to appreciate a different perspective to these vexed questions, the visit will be worthwhile.

May be the ultimate take away be the thrill of sighting a tiger in the wild, a herd of elephants, trumpeting down the wild, undisturbed herd of deer, the birds and the bees.

What motivated her to come to India? Perhaps The Mystery of the occult? Whether the 'unknown' really exists and is 'knowable' or is it confined to philosophical discussion in the psychology seminars. Often she felt somewhat confused.

Next morning there was a gentle knock at her door. There was a youngster smartly dressed who greeted her and said that he was there with the Gypsy to take her around the Park. I never realized that there are gypsies around. May be they were better guides to the forest like the Masais of Masaimara. Why did you leave the Gypsy behind? No vehicles are permitted beyond the reception unless it's an emergency, so I have parked it in the parking lot. You will have to take the trouble of walking up to the parking place. This was her second faux pass. She realized that like Falcon or Beetle it was a vehicle.

Similar thing had happened yesterday. She said most of the resorts around were named after animals. Tiger's Den, Elephant's tusk, Lion's Lair etc. but jaguar was misspelt as Jagar, yet the signage was prominently displayed. She wasn't aware that the park apart from tigers had Jaguars as well. She was told it was not misspelt. Jagar was a resort, not named after any animal, but a shamanic kind of old ritual, which was more of music and dance event in the rural areas of the region to propitiate and appease the local gods.

There is a plethora of local gods and goddesses Gram Devata- Village deity, Kul Devata-family deity, Sthan Devata-the local deity and a host of other tutelary divinities, benevolent and malevolent both. The early gods were symbols of forces of nature. Religious thought had grown from animistic and totemist traditions to non-dualistic idealistic philosophies.

In Jagar, shaman like ritual the person gets possessed by the deity and as the medium of the deity, while singing and dancing to the beat of drums thereby appeasing the deity reveals the cause of any illness, trouble or pain.

She has had her breakfast and was now all ready to enter 'the tiger territory'.

As soon as they entered the protected zone inside the park, they were able to sight a herd of spotted deer, oblivious of the human intrusion in their territory. They had got so used to the human presence, that the normal shyness of an animal in the wild had disappeared. She asked Bhaskar, the driver cum guide as to whether the tiger also behaved differently in a protected area. It's a real royal animal, the Royal Bengal Tiger he said. It all depends on its mood. There are times when it could be very elusive and at other it may totally ignore your presence. After all with royal lineage it is the king of the forest, zealously guarding its territory. Here the 'law of the jungle prevails'. It was an animals reserve, and their rights took priority over the humans often leading to man animal conflict.

For Bhaskar, hierarchy of the denizens of the park was very well defined. Royal Bengal Tiger, the king was at the top, zealously guarding its territory. Next in the hierarchy were leopards and elephants and perhaps crocodile. Then there were lesser mortals like wild boar, deer, antelopes, yellow throated martens etc. For majority of tourists birds, reptiles, insects and the flora held no attraction. There were a few rare ones, who thought in terms of a whole eco-system along with its rich bio diversity.

Sighting of a tiger depends on your luck as well as the luck and skill of the guide. Tiger in any case is the vehicle of goddess Durga, the goddess of power, said Bhaskara. Only someone superhuman has the capacity to ride it. Any clue anywhere remotely linked with psychology set her thinking. After all she was from a land which historically has been called 'Das Land der Dichter und Denker'-country of poets and thinkers.

Tigers, the favorite target for the hunters of the yesteryears was now being marketed in its living mode as a eco-tourism product. Although the park was supposed to be a conservation reserve responding to the environmental concerns of the modern era, vanishing breed of tigers, tourism as a bye-product had become important commercial proposition. Nature willy-nilly had always been commodified.. It was always reckoned as a very powerful force approached with a sense of awe, wonderment, reverence and caution. Over the years with technological success, humans thought that nature could be brought under subjugation, and reverence and caution thrown to the winds. It always proved that it was too great a force to be ignored and sidelined, leave alone the idea to subjugate it.

Brushing aside these stray thoughts, she was more interested in Bhaskar's stories- anecdotal or real she couldn't discern. It was about some of brave courageous people and their survival stories. Bhaskar was very assertive about one of his village elders, who as a well built courageous youngster encountered a leopard and wrestled with it to save his life. He successfully slayed the big cat, but was badly injured. Luckily he survived the duel and still carries the scars in his body. Life is rather harsh in remote hill villages. It gets further constrained if the wild cats from the forest neighborhood start taking interest in your activities and get nosey. No wonder, Corbett getting rid of man- eaters had acquired a demi-god status.

He came to Ramnagar along with an elder cousin.

This was the place where he got his driving lessons and was the proud owner of his gypsy. He was driver as well as a guide. It had been an enriching experience for him because he had been meeting visitors to the park from different nationalities. Every visitor had his own expectations from the tiger park, but sighting a tiger was the culmination of everyone's expectation.

You mentioned that you were few of the lucky ones who escaped from the village to this township. A village next to the forests with snow fed streams around, abounding in birds, wild flowers, right in the lap of nature, an idyllic setting so as to say how you could think of leaving it for a monotonous boring life here full of drudgery, asked Anna. I don't really know what village life is like in your part of the world, said Bhaskara. For a casual visitor it may be an idyllic natural setting, but for us it meant unending drudgery.

Human enterprise, Anna thought, is all about responding to challenges, learning from the past, living in the present, always optimistic about the future. What was by and large presented to you in a high end resort was a sanitized, veiled and edited version of the local culture.

They roamed around forest but the tiger was in no mood to show up. However, Bhaskar, who claimed to be a lucky mascot for his visitors, said it is definitely going to appear, because he sincerely prays to Goddess Durga every morning. His hidden charm. The prayers were answered and they spotted a tiger near a water hole. Purnahuti exclaimed Bhaskar- the final oblation in a sacrificial ritual. There the Royal was basking in its full glory and glamour near the water hole. Anna felt a strange mixture of emotions-excitem ent,happiness,apprehension, fear and delight. Overawed by the unique experience.

Bhaskar said that he was told that Corbett was an animal psychologist, not by any formal training but by experience in the wild. The naturalist in him could differentiate between the mating calls and alarm calls of the animals. He could discern whether a dog barking was trying to welcome someone, or whether it was angry, fearful or frustrated or aggressive by subtle variation in intonations. While tracing the man eaters, he had starting predicting the animal behavior. There was the story of an elusive 'temple tiger', which he could never shoot in spite of best efforts and finally resigned himself to abandon the shoot accepting the advice of a local temple priest-may be superstition or myths had a base or rationale of their own. The elusive Big Cat was under the protection of the temple goddess. More interesting was the story of "Bachelor of Pavalgarh", the longest tiger, the handsome innocent prince who not accused of killing any human was shot by Jim Corbett as a trophy hunter. This was the point of transformation in his life. A trophy hunter in the colonial British tradition, felt a sense of pride, ego satisfaction by big game hunting with the support of local villagers. She was told that many of the herbivores localized the movement in a limited territory in which they instinctively planned their hide outs, escape routes etc. The humans with their artificial weapons had never been factored in the nature's scheme of things.

Whether it was the aesthetic charm of the handsome prince or a guilt and remorse borne out of killing an innocent helpless animal, the trophy hunter henceforth became a diehard conservationist. All future targets were man-eaters, not the innocent big cats.

Trophy hunting in the colonial era was supposed to be a 'regal sport', which emphasized a cultural hegemony of colonizers over the colonized. While the local Indian ethic was of conservation and co-existence of all forms of life based on the principle of non-violence and non-injury, except perhaps for self-preservation, the whole idea of trophy hunting was more in an aggressive dominant mode, trying to establish a cultural supremacy symbolizing a right to rule, by subjugating the nature, flouting it's law of righteousness. Again, a glorification of an act prompted by the violent gene. An expression of masculinity.

Yet, she had experienced a strange indescribable feeling of joy satisfaction and inner happiness when she was inside the deep forest. Back to nature- the impressions embedded into the archetypal unconscious. The abode of great grand ancestors- hunter gatherers, so every time you are in 'Aranya'- the deep dark forest, psychically it is homecoming. No wonder, forest bathing is becoming increasingly popular.

You know, there were more than hundred thousand tigers wandering the Indian forest, a number which got reduced to about forty thousand when India became independent and trophy hunting continued unabated in the neo- colonial era along with shikar companies, commercial units facilitating hunting, till the number dwindled to two thousand in 1970. It was so alarming that it was felt that the species is likely to disappear from the planet. However, the alarm calls were responded to by the government by starting the tiger conservation project.

Anna was learning a lot about cultural complexities, ethnocentric divides and complex issues of sustainability science, where human systems interacted with natural systems leading to strange outcomes. Was she trying to read too much in simple issues? She had decided that the next morning she is going to visit

Pavalgarh to pay her homage to the 'Bachelor'.

She was a bit tired after the daylong safari, ingesting a bit of dust in the forests and some unknown pollens, energizing or debilitating she did not know. Had a hot shower, a wine followed by a light meal. She was intently watching the forest across the wall from her balcony. No chirping of birds. No rustling of leaves, yet she could hear the sounds of silence, and experience the power of darkness. The forest was much more vibrant at night. It's vibrations went beyond the senses touching some strange chord inside-ultra cognitive. Nature the conscious force, the illimitable matter energy of Shiva- the Lord auspicious in Indian parlance. The experience must have lasted for almost an hour before she finally decided to hit the bed.

This was the night of the Goddess. A shadowy figure veiled by mist or clouds in the background of snowy mountains beckoned her. She was trying to climb but felt that the legs did not have enough strength. It was rather too steep a mountain face. She started looking for an alternate route. The luminosity of the shadow was gradually increasing but the profile was not very clear. Angelic it appeared. She was getting curiouser every moment. She sensed divinity, but was unable to express it. She finally convinced herself that it was a dream sequence, and finally asked her as to why she made a veiled appearance. Came an answer in the softest voice she had ever heard, the veil of ignorance you have woven around yourself. Remove it and you are one with me.

It was Nanda Devi, Uma Parvati, daughter of the mountains, goddess of love, goddess of bliss, goddess of knowledge all combined into one. But where's your vehicle? Which are you referring to, the swan. No the tiger, which only you have the strength to ride. Well, I am never in a destructive mode with those who approach me with devotion and reverence. My blessings are always with the people who are pure in mind, and suddenly the luminous form disappeared in space. She gently opened her eyes. She did not have to pen down the details of the dream sequence because she remembered every bit of it. A habit of penning the details of her dreams to which she was going to make an exception today because in this case interpretation of dream was going to be at leisure and sequence had got etched in her memory.

She recalled the Devi Unsoeld incident whose death according to Benedict Berg was interpreted in different ways by different people. The local villagers interpretation, theistic in approach was that when Willy Unsoeld was mesmerized by the beauty of the Nanda Devi mountain peak, the Goddess consented to be born in his home, spent few years as a human not conscious of her divinity and finally planned her way back home to divine abode.

Anna was more serious about it, in spite of the realization that the dream sequences were creations of your own mind. Arguing for and against is also a good game to pass time.

She was imagining the glade of emerald grass on which emerged the mighty brave Bachelor of Pavalgarh. She had heard of people coming in contact with prophets, monks and saints who charted a new course, but here a human had been transformed by the martyrdom of an innocent tiger.

After exiting the park driving towards Pavalgarh, less than an hour's drive from Ramnagar it was a dense forest through which they were driving, fiery red flowers were blooming. 'Is it the flame of the Forest?' No its Bombax, red silk cotton tree, one of the softest cotton which the tree produces. As they approached the forest rest house at Pavalgarh, what caught Anna's attention was the massive girth of a Bombax tree. It seemed rather unusual, a different kind of flora altogether. Whether it be the tree or the tiger massivity was perhaps endemic to the area.

Corbett's India of poor starving millions had changed.

She was encountering a growing India which had still a long way to go. Food was still being cooked in wood fired clay ovens, clean toilets a luxury, archaic methods of waste disposal. On the other hand what she got familiar with the new consumer India trying to make a style statement in a sanitized and manicured cultural environment.

She had promised half of the final day to visit a neighbouring village where Bhaskar's brother had a home stay and where Bhaskar resided. With no restrictions of protected areas, she thought a familiarization to an Indian village will be more than welcome, providing a window to the non-sanitized, non-manicured version of India rural life style. There was a temple in the centre of the village. In the neighborhood of forests, the large animals visiting at night are treated as ghost having assumed an animal body. The ghost has to be driven away if they possessed a person by organizing a Jagar, Jaguar with a missing u.

Superstition also led to sensitivity to various omens, fetishisms, totemism and tobooism.

However, in spite of it all, she was totally overwhelmed by the hospitality of the simple village folk, nothing in return was expected, except perhaps a sense of gratitude.

Chapter - 3

RISHIKESH

Anna had a frugal breakfast today, just enough to break the fast, because she wanted to savour the *dhaba* food in one of the roadside eateries on the highway. The wayside rustic *dhaba* in natural environs over the years had been upgraded to highway family *dhaba*, by expanding its reach, quality of service and menu. Earlier on, it primarily catered to the truck drivers for whom it was apart from the food joint, a resting place, a second home of sorts. They drove the whole night and rested during the daytime, leaving the road open to buses and cars. There were wood framed cots with ropes around with a wooden plank which served as a table to keep the food plate and rest. Nature provided the open-air toilet with a hand pump for provision of water to bathe. The menu was limited to lentils maybe a vegetable and breads baked in clay ovens or tandoors. Smashed onion along with a chutney was all there for a salad. Some of them served pickles as well. The standard desert was the *kheer* — rice pudding with milk, cooked overnight.

The modernised version catered to a different clientele. It was the upmarket car traveller, who displayed a penchant for the ethnic. Bottled water, clean washrooms, a variety of food and furniture which could neither be termed minimalistic nor maximalist, a reasonable compromise between old and new, replaced the cots which were there only for display purposes — a relic of the past. Part of the premises were air-conditioned. With multiple categories of roadside eateries now, the traditional *dhaba* with its cots survived and catered to the truck drivers and provided them with their level of comfort.

Answering the call of nature was not in natural setting, because even the traditional ones had toilets constructed and bathing areas earmarked. However, the old metal crockery and cutlery were gradually replaced by modern disposable versions. There were eateries catering to fast foods and takeaways, tea being served in *kulhars* — disposable clay pots. The modern *dhaba* tended to be multi cuisine with the insertion of *Chindian* — Indian Chinese in their menu, chowmein, fried rice and dimsums of various kinds — steamed momos, fried momos etc.

It opened up the tradition vis-a-vis modernity debate. She thought of Hannah Arendt and her philosophical works like 'The Human Condition' and 'Between past and future'. Modernity for Hannah represented the age of mass society, victory of *animal laborans* over *homo faber*. Here homogeneity and conformity had replaced plurality and freedom. In the immediate context, the truck driver had lost his freedom to defecate in the open, in farmers' fields, on hygiene considerations. Fast food vs slow food. Savings in terms of time vis-a-vis a leisurely ride. Everything became open to debate. In a transition from a classical *dhaba* to a modern one, there had been a loss of identity. The seclusion of classic replaced by the hurly burly, the orderly disorder of crowded modern one. A more standardised approach in place of individual exclusivity in terms of its environment and products. She recalled Bhaskar's advice in all sincerity. If she wanted to experience a classical *dhaba* on its way to obsolescence with its traditional ambience or lack of it, she should not order anything other than tea, that too in a disposable cup. The foreigners, in his perception, had low immunity levels and had to follow a cautious approach. The other equally important advice was regarding having a meal at a *dhaba* where a large number of vehicles were parked. The larger numbers ensured that the food was fresh and had better hygienic standards. She was told that the drivers have their favourite eating joints, but she must insist on a place which attracted large crowds and cleaner environment. Finally, they stopped at a place just before

Haridwar, the entry point to the abode of gods. As regarding the choice of the meal, she went according to the cab driver's choice. Prem Singh advised her to order a standard *thali* — a plate consisting of lentils, cottage cheese in tomato gravy, mixed vegetables along with rice and tandoori flatbreads.

The destination Rishikesh was almost an hour's drive and the first sight of the *Ganges* at Haridwar stirred up a strange emotion in her. A river considered so sacred that millions over the years have been coming to take a dip in the holy waters to wash away their sins. According to the *vedic* text *Shatpatha Brahmin* of *Yajurveda Samhita*, *Vaivaswata Manu* the first progenitor of humans after the great flood, rode his boat to the Himalayan peaks and procreated the human race afresh. This was the place where *Daksh*, historically the first Aryan king of this region and mythologically the eldest psychic son of *Brahma* the creator, performed the sacrificial ritual in Kankhal in Haridwar, therefore it became a *devnirmit desh* — land of Gods. North of Haridwar were the heavenly regions where resided all the gods. Haridwar was also *Gangadwar* where river Ganges descended on the plains.

By afternoon, she was in Rishikesh. Her current destination, where she was to stay for five days. This was the *yoga* city of India where ancient spiritual *yog* got transformed into a sunrise industry called *yoga*. Godmen of various hues and colours emerged as captains of the industry. *Yoga* as an industry incidentally was incubated, grew and spread to far off places and spawned ancillaries like *yoga* apparel, *yoga* mats, foods and sprang all over the world in *yoga* shops. Rishikesh trained instructors, using the brand equity of the place, became successful entrepreneurs in their own countries. It was a commodity laced with spirituality offering a total therapy — physical, mental and spiritual. A wonder drug for all ailments, a panacea for all illness which plagued the individuals and human society.

In this process of modernization and commercialisation, metaphysical and spirit of philosophical base along with the epistemological framework was consigned to the scrap bin of the past and buried underground. Lure of the lucre had superceded the power of the soul and spirit.

She recalled her stay in Zurich, was again reminded that while browsing through the books in the library, she came across Hauer's view on *'Der Yoga un Lichte der Psychotherapy'* and Keyserling's much acclaimed 'The Travel Diary of a Philosopher', wherein it was stated that the new psychology was a rediscovery of what was already known by the ancient Indians. It referred to the old Indian 'science of the soul'. Hauer and Keyserling led to Jung. It was here that her interest in *yoga* was kindled. *'Der yoga ein Indisher weg Zurer Selbst* — 'an Indian way to self'. Jung was being brutally honest when he confessed that he could not comment upon the meaning of *yoga* for India because of lack of experience, but for the West with the prevalent psychic anarchy, any religious or philosophical practice amounted to a psychological discipline. He thought of it as methods of 'psychic hygiene'. *Kundalini yoga* in psychological terms was an introversion process likely to induce personality changes. The particular methods being culture specific were likely to induce 'mimetic madness' in the West. In his view, West will have to produce its own *yoga* in the course of time based on the principles of Christianity. Keyserling thought that physiologically they were all Christians whether their consciousness recognised it or not. Thus, every doctrine which continues in Christian spirit had a better chance of success and survival in the West than the profoundest doctrine of a foreign origin. This was the sort of 'philosophical parochialism' with which eminent psychologists and thinkers of the West greeted *yoga*. The need was to develop a cross cultural comparative psychology of inner experience. The foreign concept had to be presented in a language which could easily be understood, which also could be psychologically and physiologically acceptable. *ostasian denkt anders* — 'East Asia thinks otherwise' and therefore may not be replicable as such.

There were more severe critics in Germany who thought of *yoga* and *tantrism* as psycho-spiritual science fiction and sexual acrobatics that could put to shame even the most imaginative of pornographers.

Now that Anna was in the land of *yog* as well as *yoga*, she had to make her own appraisal and critical assessment, which was going to be her takeaway from this place.

Since the afternoon *dhaba* meal was slightly on the spicier side for her, she decided to visit a cafe for a lighter dinner. She entered a bookstore and what caught her interest was the book titled 'The Philosophy and Psychology of Yoga Practice' authored by Swami Krishnanand along with 'The Epistemology of Yoga' by the same author. Having purchased the books and making a mental note of a few books like 'Studies in Comparative Philosophy' and 'The Art of Total Thinking', she decided to have an early dinner in a cafe.

All meat dishes were a taboo, no German *Bratwurst*, *rindfleischwurst*, no *Schnitzel*. The choice was between vegetarian and vegan. She finally settled for a tomato, carrot, pumpkin soup along with the spinach mushroom vegan omelette pancake. She had been forewarned about avoiding the salads except in high-end star category restaurants. So, anything well-cooked was a safe bet. Looking at the menu, the breakfast menu in the cafe was rather interesting. Among the multiple choices in the breakfast menu categorized into French breakfast, Simple breakfast, Yogi breakfast, Healthy breakfast and Special breakfast apart from Vegan breakfast and Raw Vegan breakfast, the menu also offered backed beans, a misprint or perhaps fortified version of baked beans. She had the time till morning to decide about it. The city offered multiple cuisine choices, starting from Indian, Chinese, Tibetan, Nepalese, Italian, German, Continental, but without meat. Soya nuggets acted as the meat substitute.

Walking along the Ganges, she was wondering as to what made the river a living legend. She will have to look for the answers in the Indian mythology.

Thompson, the eminent English historian, was of the view that it was a paradox of history that no important people or forces in the 18th century France wanted a revolution. Revolutions begin as wars do, not because people positively want them, but such circumstances get created that lead to revolution. Subsequently, the murder of Archduke Ferdinand at Sarajevo precipitated the First World War, a clash between pan Germanism and pan Slavism, monarchy and emerging nationalism. Similarly, a kind of disillusionment among the American youth with the prevalent dominant culture in USA, a society which was perceived as a conservative capitalist and anti democratic while professing liberal democratic values, and US involvement in the Vietnam War to satisfy its neoimperialistic ambitions, triggered a counter culture movement — hippies professing liberation from an oppressive sociocultural system. A pseudo spirituality sprang from nowhere which got reflected in terms of outlandish dresses, free sex, marijuana smoking, LSD consumption and psychedelic experiences.

The new high for the hippies and the flowers generation was getting popular. Sociologists, psychologists and economists provided their own interpretation and explanation. Waste production as a result of industrial revolution, loss of identity due to cultural hegemonic decline, coupled with the sense of alienation and isolation were identified as the cause.

One of the big beneficiaries of the counter culture, a new age movement, was the sleepy little town of Rishikesh in the cradle of Himalayas. What attracted large numbers of the 'flower children' along with the Beatles — torchbearer of the rock music, along with Hollywood celebrities to this place was a pseudo spirituality or easy availability of psychotropic substances like smoking grass? This could be a matter of debate. However, the movement changed the status of the place and its claim to be *'yoga* capital of the world' the ancient Indian science and philosophy was emerging as a thriving service industry.

The age of commercial *yoga* had begun and with it, new investment opportunities in the ancillaries. The *ashrams* — the monastic setups were being upgraded to star category ascetic resorts. The daring, audacious and enterprising self-proclaimed 'godmen' felt confident enough to commodify transcendence. Transcendental meditation was being marketed by 'expert' empirical techniques. With the new influx of Westerners, the dining scene also expanded both in terms of volume and diversity.

Yogic diet was getting a new meaning. Culinary preferences were undergoing a transformation. According to Swatmarama, the author of *Hatha Yoga Pradeepika*, bitter, sour, pungent, saltish, hot, green vegetables, fermented, oily, mixed with till seed, rapeseed, intoxicating liquors, fish, meat, curds, buttermilk, kulattha pulses, plum, asafoetida, garlic, onion etc. were classified as foods injurious to a *Yogi*. Ayurveda had its own definition of healthy and unhealthy foods and even advocated meat broth for certain kinds of fever. However, Rishikesh being declared a pilgrim centre, liquor and meat including fish was placed in a prohibited category, even though *soma* extraction and offering had been eulogized in the *vedic* treatises. New culinary preferences were emerging keeping the foreigners' palate in mind. Influx of foreigners and interest shown in *yoga*, gave ethnicity a boost. To have an ethnic orientation in lifestyle was becoming a fashion statement. It was more a lip service than a genuine desire to follow the cultural traditions. Elite taking to a hitherto neglected discipline, just because it was being somewhat sanctified and patronized by the West. *Ayurveda*, the *upveda* of *Vedas* along with astrology, a limb of Vedas were assuming new dimensions, finding its linkage with *yoga* — the sunrise industry. Ayurveda massages, *panchakarma*, the forgotten techniques were emerging in its new *avatar*, assuming new forms along with the rising tide of *yoga*. Here economics had started guiding the sociocultural tradition.

Anna just browsed through one of the books she had bought yesterday regarding the psychology of *yoga*. It gave her a new insight into Indian psychology. She went to the cafe where she had her meal last night. For breakfast, she finally decided in favour of a healthy combination of bread slices with peanut butter, muesli, fruit curd, mixed fruit juice and green tea. The *yogi* breakfast over which she preferred the healthy one consisted of cheese toast, fruit salad, curd, juice and '*yogi tea*' — whatever it meant, maybe some sort of a herbal concoction. After a walk along the banks of Ganges she went back to the bookstore from where she had purchased the books yesterday. Today she picked up '*Synthesis of Yoga*' by Aurobindo. She asked for the bookshop owner's advice as to the ashrams she should be visiting while in Rishikesh. Two places were suggested by him to begin with. One was supposed to be in the classical mould where over the years footfall had decreased and which, for the modern visitors, had become archaic. The other was the one patronised by the foreigners and the Indian elite

— the new millionaires for whom ethnicity was a part of the style statement, the new bourgeoisie who had to appear different from the commoners. An interesting viewpoint, she thought. Took the directions, fed the locations in her mobile and walked to the reception of the old one to seek appointment with someone who could give her an insight into the history and activities of the *ashram*. The person at the reception had a friendly disposition and guided her to one of the inmates who, apart from being a yoga instructor, was keenly involved in the management of the *ashram*. It was a rather candid discussion on the transformation of values with time. "We have become archaic, obsolete and irrelevant not because we have changed, but because in general perception, we continue in the classical mode which is outdated. We still stick to the first generation or second generation mobiles in a world where the third and fourth generations would be entering in near future. We, the followers of *Vedanta* philosophy feel like gravitating towards Buddha's doctrine where he said that there is nothing permanent in this world. Everything is in a flux. All movement, everything transient. Each new technological innovation has a shrinking life cycle. In an evolutionary cycle where there is a constant struggle for existence and only the fittest survives, we are not sure whether we are the wise ones or idiots of the first order sticking to our 'doctrine of being'. There came the hippies who with easy availability of grass in the land of Lord Shiva which opened their third eye and were followed by yuppies. For a while, spirituality became a new buzzword. It opened the eyes of various adventurous, enterprising masters to the emerging market in the West. While hippies were heading eastwards, the godmen titled as Gurus, non-Gurus and non-Guru Gurus were heading westwards trying to work out collaborative arrangement, mutually beneficial. Our adventurous audacious brethren thought that transcendental could be objectified and marketed provided you received the right price. Meditation was selling as 'cup of tea meditation' as one of the masters remarked. What a travesty of concept 'truth' which Acharya Vidyaaranya had said was a concept which was incontradictable. Truth, transcendence self, were no longer trans-empirical concepts. Everything had a price, preferably in a dollar denomination. What first appeared as a whiff of fresh air from the West had brought along a new set of consumers. To our surprise, one day a visitor walked into our *ashram* inquisitive about the price for a six-month-long training course on *sanyasa*. He had brought with him a brochure about a year-long course on '*sanyasa*' at a fairly reasonable price. The person was keen about short term courses.

"*Varnashram* was part of the Indian socio-cultural and philosophical systems. *Chaturashramya* starts with the austere ideal of *brahmacharya*, discipleship with the sense of dedication and devotion to the teacher, *grihastha* — the normal householders life to fulfil the social obligations in accordance with the moral and ethical precepts, leading to retirement or *vanprastha* where one disassociates himself with an active life of production and reproduction yet maintaining social relationships in a positive frame of mind. Then comes *Sanyasa*— a sense of detachment and preparation of final journey. Historians say that this system though considered ideal from a social and philosophical view was violated all through. But what survived was the concept of '*satyamev jayate na anratam*' and '*satyam gyanam anantam brahma*' — truth infinite prevails, not falsehood."

"So, all these distortions, I view as a temporary setback. Some of the modern great Indian masters in their innovative genius, alchemists of the century had for a while obliterated the distinction between natural and supernatural, between physical and metaphysical and had overruled sage Yagyavalkya's dictum *vigyataram are kena vijaniyat*. Supreme felicity of plenum beyond cognition, perception, mentation and understanding could be offered on a golden platter provided one was willing to pay the right price. The strength of the Indian culture, spirituality being at the core of it, is the resilience. Soon a disillusionment set in among the new visitors. No wonder when the master asked The Beatles as to why they were leaving, one of them cryptically or sarcastically remarked that you should be knowing it better because you are the cosmic one.

"However, the echo of spirituality which came back from the West had carried with it the bug of consumerism. The more discerning masters who had a penchant for commerce started heading West viewing it as a land of opportunities. Among them were a few who sincerely wanted to convey the message of spirituality to the West, but their number was small. Larger were those who had the skills to manipulate the system to their advantage — pragmatic, daring and willing to take risks with an intuitive sense of the hidden potential of consumer *yoga*. The fundamental difference between *yoga* and *yog* was the reversal of technique. While in *yog* an individual got transformed into universal by an internalising process, here the individual masters were becoming universal by an external process of globalization in *yoga*. Moreno, the founder of Psychodrama conceived it as a theatre of spontaneity with therapeutic effects. He once told Dr Freud that 'I start where you leave off. You meet people in artificial settings of your office. I meet them on the street and their homes in their natural surroundings. You analyse their dreams. I give them the courage to dream again. You analyse and tear them apart. I let them act out their conflicting roles and help them put the parts back together again.' He initially gathered a group of prostitutes, discussed their problems, and with the experience started the psychodrama".

"But when East entered West with new age masters, there emerged the 'crazy wisdom' to awaken consciousness. Sacred became profane, spirituality transformed into unspiritual mundane. Sexecology became part of the transpersonal psychology. 'Garbage and the Goddess' — a sexual theatre was the symbol of the decade. I purposely used the word 'decade' because these distortions normally do not last more than a decade. Like fashion in clothing, they change very fast. Buzz words disappear in the thin air.

"Mysticism had not been our monopoly, whereas perhaps *yoga* was. But ours were first among the mystics preceding Plato and said Swami Krishnanda, liberal, scholarly master of old school, supremely catholic in his approach found Plotinus's neo-platonism nothing short of 'Advaita Vedanta of Shankara', the foundation for which had been laid by the likes of Sage Yagyavalkya. Only the view that the world is an overflow of the perfection of God was peculiar to Plotinus, for in Vedanta, it is absolute and world is an appearance — illusory or otherwise.

There was Heraclitus among the first western philosophers to go beyond the physical theory in search of metaphysical foundations and moral applications".

"You said you had come from Germany? Are you familiar with Master Eckhart"? "Only to the extent that he had been one of the German mystics, a Catholic theologist who wrote in German vernacular language." "You know in India also, Vedic Sanskrit was different and post Panini the grammarian, Sanskrit was different. The human quest for truth, distortions here and there notwithstanding was the same.

The threefold clasp we cannot grasp The circle's span no mind can scan For here is a mystery fathomless

It is there, it is here, it's far it's near It's high, its low, yet all we know is This is not, that is not.

Now *Ishopanishad* says, it is static as well as dynamic, it is very far yet very near. So, says Yagyavalkya, it is neither small nor big, neither gross nor subtle. *Neti Neti* not this, not this".

The conversation was getting very interesting. She had already decided to postpone her visit to commercial yoga centre, an ashram which claimed to have the highest footfall.

"In the West out of dissatisfaction with the socio-economic system and concomitant cultural norms, and a demand grew for instant solutions — pseudo psycho-spiritual remedies, and enterprising *yoga* merchants were willing to dilute the spiritual content. A rather pragmatic approach catering to market demand, discarding the accepted value systems and standards. Sacred becoming profane, and spirituality going mundane was okay as long as it reaped in the moolah and ego of the supplier got a boost".

"Holderin said, *Liko Gefahr ist, Wachst das Retende auch* — 'where there is a danger, the saving thing also grows'. In the nearby region, there grows a grass called stinging nettle. You touch it and the skin starts itching and paining. Next to it a wild spinach like grass grows which mitigates it. There was in the earlier century, a great spiritual teacher called Swami Vivekananda who, according to his guru, Sri Ramakrishna, was born with a divine mission, arrived uninvited and unannounced at the Chicago Parliament of Religions and took the parliament by storm. He professed *Vedanta* — 'the voice of freedom'. "Another flag bearer of Indian culture of spirituality, who was the most unique and fascinating character of orthodox Hindu philosophy was Sri Aurobindo. An iconoclast who came with a message gleaned from the *Upanishads* that self is an Ens which is not knowable by sight or any of the senses, it can only be grasped in the innate conception 'I am'. He had absolutely no hesitation to announce that *Vedantisms* had long time back mastered physical and psychical laws which science is now beginning to handle".

Among the stalwarts, I have had the good fortune of meeting here in Rishikesh a professed theologian, brilliant scholar, profound philosopher and a prolific writer, a great yogi by the name of Swami Krishnanand. All distortions to the philosophy of *yoga* were temporary and he kept the flag flying on the philosophical front of *yoga* and *Vedanta* with his knowledge, extreme liberal outlook and Catholic approach".

"Although our Guru–disciple relationship never got formalised, I have had the privilege of interacting with him on philosophy related issues and learnt my first lessons on *yoga*. By a heroic attitude and courageous mind, an aspirant by restraining the mind by taking it into confidence and obtaining its voluntary compliance for self-control, melting it into the self attains a blissful state. Extreme happiness as experienced by higher purified reason intrinsically good going beyond the 'pleasant' of sense is this. It is total union with self and the separation of consciousness from all sources of pain".

"Humans, he felt suffered because of a double whammy. First the metaphysical one, immortal unlimited universal unity from infinite to a particularised finite partite limited individual subject to pain, grief and mortality. The second on a psychological earthly level.Humanity in a very important sense could be regarded as a 'wholly brainwashed species indoctrinated from childhood' with mind prejudiced by various divides on grounds of nationality, race, colour, sects, language, class, family and many other groups. These social constructs promoted a sense of ego, individual or collective, divided rather than united. This divisive selfishness stems from certain historical forces unleashed by nature. Basic instinct of psycho-physical survival leads to attachment, jealousy and fear. *Raga, dvesh* and *abhinivesh* as Patanjali viewed the *klesh* or painful afflictions".

"That is why the battleground of *Kurukshetra* in *Mahabharat* symbolises an 'arena that this world is, a house disjointed against itself. The separative consciousness where 'seer' is not willing to identify himself with the 'seen' but prefers to dominate by considering it inferior leading to a struggle and this confrontation defines all life. The good and evil are all here. The high and low, great and small are all within this battlefield. Men kill men by waging wars, but wars are waged for peace of men. Contradiction is life on earth. It is hard to know what is right and wrong. To throw the bow and arrows down in resentment through confusion and by wrenching oneself from the whole is not a cure to the aches of life.

It had been a very satisfying experience and she scheduled another visit for the next day. The commercial institution could wait or even skipped.

Next days discussion veered around the philosophical interpretations of yoga and vedanta and it's validity and relevance in the modern day environment. Here again eulogising Swami Krishnananda, the Ashram inmate extensively quoted him. He was of the view that majority of the people in a monastic set up think that they are religious seekers, spiritual aspirants, disciples of gurus, but we have to be very realistic about the world around. We don't live in a world of spirituality. It's a chaotic world full of disharmony, quarrel and battles.

It's not hunky dory all around. It's a world of harsh reality. World is like a battlefield where a bow may twang or a machine gun may fire any moment. However on a deeper analysis our problems do not come from the world but are of own making. Our problem emerges from our psyche, when we find it difficult to reconcile to the outside world as it exists, Our ego sense urges us to behave in a manner where our opinion, our views, our judgement should prevail over everybody else's.

This is what makes the task of impartial and objective self analysis very arduous. That's why the analogy of walking on the razors edge or on burning embers is often justified. Is there a way out?

Yes, says the Master. The arduous task is to find the oasis in this desert like world. It starts by a change in our psyche by gradual neutralisation of our ego and subsequent realization that comes from our inner voice that we have a capacity which is much more than what normally appears to be. We have an element in us, which goes beyond this sensory phenomenal world. We have to rise to a philosophical realm, much above the normal worldly realm. Self analysis, self realization and self discovery starts by acceptance of our hidden potential- the oasis. We must become conscious of the fact that the world has a purpose. It's a teleological march towards a destination. It is an evolutionary scheme of things, where we are marching forward, and the process can be fast tracked. Our intellectual analysis has to be gradually superceded by a deeper philosophical perspective, where we enter into the world of intuitive wisdom, by recognition of the trans empirical domain. A herculean task, a total transformation in the way we think, act and behave.

Master said that life is neither science nor logic, it's a tremendous mystery. It is a miracle which keeps us hoping and living. Religion is pursuing the Holy Grail of this wondrous mystery, unravelling the treasure house that it is. Religious adventure is spiritual adventure, going beyond rituals and liturgy. It opens the gates to universal compresence, beyond individual existence.

It had been rather dense even for a person who was well versed with principles of psychology, with a wide academic and research experience. She needed time for it to seep in. No more visits to any other place. Henceforth, it was going to be a reflection on whatever she had imbibed. Rishikesh had already paid it's dividend. Perhaps, it had initiated her into a new way of thinking.

Chapter - 4

ON TO HARSHIL

Having left behind Corbett with its wildlife and Rishikesh with its assumed spirituality, Anna was on her way to Tripatha Ashram in Harshil Village in the Uttarkashi District of Uttarakhand in the central Himalayan region. The winding narrow road without crash barriers and parapets at most places and deep ravines and gorges were giving her a constant fright. A Freudian, she knew how to differentiate between Furcht (fear) and Schreck (fright). Fright set in when you encountered danger without being prepared for it. God forbid, if the driver lost his control on the wheel, she may ultimately land up paying a rather heavy price for her lessons on contemplative psychology.

Why did she at all let a negative thought enter her mind. It had been more than three hours since she started her journey from Rishikesh and had almost covered more than one third of the distance. She decided to make some polite conversation with the driver. Before coming to India she had taken a few lessons in Hindi. The driver assured her that this road was like child's play for him, because he had driven on narrower and much more dangerous roads..Whenever his confidence wavered his strategy to emerge out of it was by saying his prayers sincerely. Faith had always been on his side, because he always thought positive. Moreover, they were on their way to a pilgrim place in the land of gods, so gods will take care of them. She thought of the buses plunging into the river and people bidding goodbye to this world, even though imbued with faith fortified by prayers. The driver had an explanation for that. Often it was the casual approach of the driver, drunken driving or mechanical failure. But at the end of the day, the law of Karma was in operation. The Karmik theory needs to be understood better. So strongly was it imbued in the Indian psyche that rebirth also resulted as a consequence. It determined the quality of life. For the time being, the drivers self confidence and cool demeanor was quite reassuring and suddenly she became aware of the flowering red rhododendrons and wild daisies and lilies on the hill sides. She looked at the terraced fields on the villages where she noticed a stream in the valley below. The driver during the course of conversation had mentioned that while entering the abode of gods, the Himalayas, he got imbued with Shraddha which was also his protective armour. It was a Sanskrit word which like many others had no exact English equivalent, but conveyed a sense of faith, humility, reverence and devotion. Yet another word added to her long list which needed a detailed explanation. Sanskrit, she was told by a priest in Rishikesh, was the language of gods, which implied purity and refinement. Often a word in Sanskrit had multiple meanings depending on the context. A number of key words relevant to philosophy and psychology had no exact equivalents in other languages.

Was it drivers simple ideas of religiosity, faith etc. or the cathartic impact of mother nature in her glory she decided temporarily to send her sense of rationality for a short sabbatical and was more than willing to interact with the flowers, trees and grass which all appeared to be sentient and inviting and she was more than willing to respond.

Ideas of pre-existence of soul and post mortem existence, herein before and herein after of life, destiny chance, coincidence, teleology and eschatology, which all along had been an anathema to her thoroughly rationalist psyche were surreptitiously trying to gain an entry into it and unwittingly she welcomed it albeit temporarily. Perhaps more was in store for her.

The same forbidding landscape dominated by rock face and deep dangerous gorges which was frightening her half an hour back was now offering bounties of nature-pleasurable, aesthetic. The mind had changed its orientation. Mind a perennial problem? Creator of illusions or reality? Gross or subtle? Undefined, interpreted in a hundred ways. Neurologist, psychologist, philosopher, materialist and idealist they all had their own definitions – the truth of mind and sanctity of each interpretation zealously guarded. For her it was a particular condition of the psyche at a particular time and with close linkages with the neural system, of course with unparalleled wanderlust.

Meanwhile they had arrived at the halfway point on top of the ridge, where the driver stopped for his afternoon cup of tea and snack. She got out of the car and the snow white peaks of the Himalayas were in full view in front of her. Thousands of rock and soil risen from the Sea of Tethys over forty million years covered by snow, glistening white in the sunshine. It was awe inspiring, mesmerizing to say the least. The massivity, the humongousness and the glory overtook her completely at first sight. It was somewhat distant yet no near. She was tempted to start a conversation with the mountains. She was suddenly reminded of Surya Greens 'The call of the Sun a woman's journey to the heart of wisdom'. A travel writer who was introduced by the rising sun to a subtle language and then began her interactions with sun. What started for her in Pondicherry Ashram and continued in Benaras was her awareness of sun as a living being. Anna had dismissed it as utter nonsense, a gimmick to attract the gullible readers. Suddenly it made an altogether different sense to her. Here was the glorious white mountain beckoning her - the call of the mystique? She just wanted to be embraced in its arms, in total blissful solitude. Momentarily the difference between sentient and insentient had got obliterated. She never gave much thought initially to transpersonal psychology, PSI and paranormal experience till she heard the story of Devi Unsoeld from Benedikt. Was it her brush with the occult, which her rational mind had dismissed all along. Her world by and large had revolved around conscious, sub-conscious and unconscious, id and ego. Grudgingly she had accepted Jung's idea of archetypal unconscious.

The driver before his afternoon snack, followed a footpath close to the forest and she instinctively followed him to a small temple close by. She was told that all local drivers invariably paid their obeisance there to the god thereby ensuring a safe and secure journey. Nestled among the oak and Rhododendron trees, the temple had an idol of Lord Shiva in Linga form, a visible symbol of an invisible force. After washing her hands, she entered the small temple and closed her eyes. It was a momentary contemplation. Was it the aroma of the incense sticks or some strange kind of vibration which again resulted in a state of momentary bliss. No words, no sound, absolute silence, peace all around. A strange feeling of psychological holism, where all the activities of the mind had ceased for a while. With eyes closed and palms folded perhaps it was her first brush with divinity invoking a sense of spirituality, a strange feeling of divine presence. These were perhaps matters of faith which did not follow rational logic. It was not the stone idol, which was being worshipped, but the idea of pure consciousness symbolized by the deity. Deity in the ultimate sense is the idea which is found to be fit to be worshipped. A supreme idea, a state of consciousness beyond the ken of our empirical categories of understanding, which becomes easier to identify if, characterized by a symbol.

There was a signage next to the temple quoting Skanda purana, a mythological text that the glories of Himalayas cannot be described in a thousand ages of gods. As the morning dew is dried up by the morning sun, so are the sins of mankind by the sight of Himalayas.

It was the presumed presence of gods, noble souls of sages and seers and ascetic saints and legendary allusions to all that was holy, pious and sacred, which had influenced the Indian psyche over the ages and had sanctified every rock, stone, tree, mountain, river stream and the region as a whole. No wonder that in the ancient past people even in the old age imbued with faith after bidding farewell to their near and dear ones undertook tedious journeys to the pilgrim destination through the mountain footpaths, walking hundreds of miles lacking all modern conveniences to pay their respect to revered god and goddesses.

With the hypnotic influence of the awe-inspiring snowy mountains getting somewhat diluted, pangs of hunger had started raising their head.

Close to the temple was the roadside eatery, where a stray dog wagging his tail in anticipation of food was there to welcome her. She rested her haunches on a wooden bench. Without caring much about the hygiene of the place, she thought that she would settle for a plate of instant noodles. However, the buttery aroma of paratha- potato stuffed flatbread being shallow fried in clarified butter was irresistible. Enthused by the driver Prem Singh's choice she took the risk of ordering it. The frugal but delicious lunch snack was followed by a very sugary concoction by the name of tea to which ginger had been added.

Hunger being taken care of, halfway mark crossed descent had begun and with it the excitement of being closer to the destination. An unknown destination which you have not visited before is like future where you have the liberty to speculate, imagine and fantasize. She knew that the fundamental principle of yoga was to curb the wanderlust of mind, a much-maligned organ in Yoga parlance, except for the anatomists.

Anatomist realized that human body was a piece of bad design engineering from Homo erectus onwards. One had to balance a body with high centre of gravity on the small surface area of one's feet. However, the mind a euphemism for brain as part of the central nervous system was the balancing factor. Any injury to that part meant that a person fell on all his fours. This was the indispensability of mind for all conscious activities. Minus mind in operation you were either in deep sleep or perhaps swoon. She had limited time before she entered the monastic discipline of an ascetic retreat. She now had the freedom of mind to roam around all over the universe, open herself to invasion of thoughts of all kind, divine undivine, sacred profane. She had become oblivious to the presence of the driver. She wondered whether Yoga was a path to divinity or just an escape route to rid yourself of worries and hassles of workaday world.

The psychologist in her mind raised its head. It is always a small insignificant ripple in the mind which leads to either pleasure or pain. The externally perceived world, the physical nature harbouring all the objects provides the stimulus, which most of time goes unnoticed, unattended to only become the building blocks of the dream world.

She recollected that Freud had lamented that while we should willingly acknowledge any philosophical or psychological theory that could tell us the meaning of feelings of 'pleasure' and 'pain' which affect us so powerfully, yet no theory of any value is forthcoming. In the absence of such a theory, it got linked to the quantity of excitation present in the psychic experience, pain corresponding to increase and pleasure to decrease in the quantity.

With a limited exposure yet to the basic concept of Indian philosophy of Yoga and Vedanta she thought, it was very unfortunate for the knowledge community as such that most of the path breakers in philosophy and psychology in the west belonged to an era when internet was not available. Greats like Freud, Jung, Adler, could not even virtually interact with the interpreters of two great psycho analysts and philosophers of India, sage Patanjali proponent of Raj Yoga and Sage Krishna Dvaipayana Vyas author of Gita.

She was yet to be initiated into the Indian tradition where psychology in its transpersonal dimensions had not been delinked with a philosophy which could not be conceived without its concomitant metaphysics. While Western psychology gradually disassociating its linkage with philosophy gravitated more towards life sciences, the ancient Indian tradition was firmly rooted in metaphysics and spirituality. Philosophy here meant a vital content of consciousness in its generality, addressing fundamental question of birth, life, death, afterlife, metempsychosis, rebirth and universe trying to find the best possible solutions to the riddle of life and universe in an inclusive manner.

With eyelids closed she surrendered herself to sleep and woke up after a while realizing that the car had come to a stop, because of a temporary road jam. A few boulders had slid down the hillside, and a bulldozer was at work clearing the debris. The driver informed her that it might take half an hour before the road is opened to traffic. She got off the vehicle and started loitering around. Fortunately, it was a cloudy afternoon and the heat was bearable.

They were now driving along the major tributary of the Holy Ganges, Bhagirathi originating from Gomukh, Cow's mouth glacier and would be meeting its younger sister Alaknanda a few kilometers down the stream, the confluence place called Dev Prayag-confluence of the celestials. However, the river in its own identity was fully satisfied as the daughter of the Himalayas. The flow was fast, the undercurrents would be faster, flowing towards its destination ocean where it was going to lose its individual identity or gain a much larger identity, depending on one's own perspective. That's how Yoga was defined, shedding individual ego to embrace the universal. The flowing waters represented a continuous change which incidentally was the main pastime or rather the normal tendency of the human mind. The challenge is to organize and elevate it with effort and perseverance so that it acquiesces and submits itself to self-enlargement and self-improvement. Like the turbulent waters of the river below it doesn't submit itself to control so easily.

Meanwhile she was informed that the debris had been cleared, the muck disposed of by throwing it into the river below and they could proceed. The stream of thought broken, she went back to her seat.

For her the surface view of the flowing river and the movement thereof had been easy to discern, but to understand the undercurrents and turbulence therein, one would have to dive deep, fraught with a risk element and danger. A proper diving equipment along with other safety aids were needed, Aids to Yoga, as they say, the moral observances, cleansing processes, rational discernment between the essentials and non-essentials, eternal existent and the transient.

The driver was lamenting that it was a chronic slip zone where almost every season at the slightest rain, landslides occurred, but none of the authorities ever cared to find a lasting solution. It was always crisis management with temporary solutions which involved waste of time and energy besides avoidable inconvenience to the passengers.

She made a mental reference to a book on 'Indian Psychology' which in the path of yoga delineated a course where in you had to go to the basic cause of the problem, like a doctor investigating to diagnose a health problem and once the cause was rightly ascertained the remedy became an easy affair. However in a world of fast foods, robots and artificial intelligence, time, effort and perseverance were in short supply. Rough and ready temporary solutions were easier to come by.

Although the wait seemed to be painful from the drivers point, she was engrossed in her mental interaction with the holiest of holy rivers of India. Ganga originating from the lotus feet of Vishnu the sustainer entered the earth through the matted locks of Shiva like the slender thread of lotus flower.

The small rivulets and tributaries, insignificant in themselves, attained a distinct larger entity by merging with the Ganges. The rivers treated as a curse like Tamsa also became sacred by surrendering their individual identity to the Holy Ganges.

A few stops where the driver voluntarily stopped the car, paid his reverence by folding his hands were the sites where some accident or mishap had occurred. Small temples had been erected by the roadside housing the gods, which perhaps were like strong force fields to ward off all demonic and destructive powers.

They were the presiding principle of all that was sacred, divinity always battling the profane. The local deity, though low in hierarchy than the pan-Indian gods, were supposed to exert a greater influence in the local area and therefore were feared as well as revered. Lord Krishna in his discourse in Gita had been very liberal to the devotees by saying that a leaf, a flower, fruit or even water was as valuable an offering as any. It was the spirit of devotion which mattered rather than the material offerings. The driver told Anna that he always carried with him on a long journey, small denomination coins to be offered at different temples. When asked whether it not amounted to bribing the god, he was visibly upset. In a somewhat remonstrative manner, he said that whatever I have has been given by him so it's just a token of my respect for him. I cannot even dream of repaying his debt. All liturgical practices irrespective of religious denomination are symbolic of faith, a silent expression of the sprit, which cannot be valued in material terms. While making an offering, blessings are sought in return. Faith and devotion like 'qualia' can never be quantified in material terms. It was somewhat of a philosophical discourse from her point of view. She realized each deity, apart from being a supernatural entity and deified force on utilitarian plane, also represented a manifestation of the non-dual Absolute. It is the divinity within our hearts which attracts us to our own created anthropomorphic gods. The great learning experience for her in last few days was that it is the divinity perceived to be outside urging the divine within us to unite.

They had now entered the verdant valley of Harshil decorated with Deodar, the tree of gods and Blue Pine and surrounded by majestic snow-covered peaks. She again felt like a child in the warm embrace of Mother Nature, the original creatrix. Nature attracts us because our roots lie there, Guna Guneshu Vartante – It's the principle of gravity the force of attraction because the elements which constitute our psycho-physical personality, also constitute the physical nature.

The Tripatha Ashram, her final destination today was situated in the valley of Harshil on the banks of Jalandhari, a tributary of Bhagirathi, according to mythology, the ever turbulent Jalandhari and mighty Bhagirathi vied with each other for supremacy and Lord Vishnu settled the dispute by establishing himself as a Shila or rock in Harshil. Tripatha - the legend of Ganges also derived its name from mythology – a river which flowed in heavens had to descend to earth because of a curse and even had to flow in the nether world, taking three different paths, and out here retaining her sanctity as the goddess, daughter of the mountain Lord Himalaya.

The person who received her at a makeshift kind of reception wasn't saffron clad for a change. Benedikt had already given her low down on the place which she was to experience in the coming days.

She was ushered to her cabin, neat and clean, sparsely furnished with a copy of Shrimad Bhagwat Gita in English translation kept there. Since she had had her meal on the way, she preferred to rest for a while and sought an appointment with Rohitashwa, an inmate of the ashram in the evening. Confirming what Benedikt had said, her first impression about the place was that the place did not have the usual formal trapping of a monastery.

When she met Rohitashwa in the evening and addressed him as Swamiji. He politely told her to drop the title, because Swami means an owner the Lord- and we are all our own lords governed by a supreme lord, and that's why every person here was addressed by their names. It often refers to a teacher who has been initiated into renunciation.

Coming to name, Rohitashwa symbolised the energy of the sun- its seven horses pulling the chariot in its journey in space. She never gave a thought to the significance of a name but was to realize later that names in India had a special significance, often based on Rashi the moon sign, the Indian Counterpart of Zodiac signs, sun being replaced by moon. It related to the cosmic conditions as evinced by the planetary position and constellations at the time and place of birth. The underlying logic of Indian astrology was that in the cosmic process everything was linked with each other so a name in consonance with the moon sign harmonized the personality with cosmic conditions. Naming ceremony was a ritual. A practice which gradually was being discarded with the new generation looking for novelty, rather than meaning and significance of names much to the consternation of the astrologers, a vanishing breed, unable to acclimatise to the new environment.

While taking a short stroll on the premises of the retreat the person receiving her asked her about her journey. A mountain journey is rather tiring because you do not traverse a straight path at the same elevation. There are ascent and descent, twists and turns, curves and bend, towering peaks and precipices.

Yoga incidentally is like that, where you gradually try to ascend to the peak, but there are ridges in between. The destination appears to near while you are negotiating a ridge only to discover a few more in between which were not visible initially. A situation which most of the mountaineers understand quite well. Effort and perseverance therefore are the key. It tires you out, takes every ounce of energy, yet the very sight of destination fills you up with reserve. Mountaineers have the skills to negotiate the crevices, rock faces, avalanches with a burning desire to reach the summit with reverence to the mountains.

Skill in action coupled with equanimity is one of the numerous definitions of yoga as enunciated in Gita.

After a frugal vegetarian meal of rice, lentils, and mixed vegetables along with a cucumber salad and rice pudding, she retired to bed early. For a while, after she had closed her eyes, she felt that she was still being driven on the winding roads and clutching to the seat handle as if it is going to be her saviour. But sleep came early and she had temporarily retired to a state of involuntary unconsciousness.

She woke up in the morning to the chirping of birds, came out of her cabin and looked at the snowcapped peaks around. She was perhaps rather tired last evening to appreciate the beauty of nature.

She was keenly looking forward to her lessons on Indian psychology which had close linkage with philosophy. Psychology divorced from philosophy did gravitate towards science newly found beau ideal in the west, where specialization and compartmentalization ruled over the idea of integrality and inclusivity. Will Durant had lamented that human knowledge had become too great for human mind leading to a scientific specialist who knew more and more about less and less and philosophical speculator who knew less and less about more and more.

Lest Jung be accused of gender bias in his outlining the spiritual problem of the modern man, she interpreted 'man' included 'women', a psychologist's bias prevailing over the gender identity, perhaps her quest was for answers which lay within the domain of spirituality. She still had an ambivalent attitude towards Jung's dictum 'that fascination the soul had for modern consciousness, was the kernel of the present spiritual problem.' A pessimistic view would treat it as sign of decay, while an optimist view would find a germ of a deep change in West's attitude towards spirituality.

She decided to engage Rohitashwa once she met him in a conversation on this issue. To her queries about spirituality and Jung's viewpoint, Rohit came out with an interesting story of Trishanku.

Trishanku the king, a denizen of earth, was keen to ascend to heavens along with his physical body, which was clearly a transgression of laws of nature. The story finds mention in the epic Ramayana, a saga of Lord incarnate Ram. He approached sage Vasistha, the wise one to perform a sacrificial ritual which would catapult him to an exalted position in heaven along with the mortal body intact. The wise sage expressed his inability to do so. He tried to pressurize his sons who cursed him to lose his kingship and get to a wretched condition. In tattered clothes, he approached Vasishtha's rival sage Vishwamitra, who to prove his superiority used his mystical powers to send him heaven wards.

The gods did not appreciate it, and the king of gods Indra used his godly powers to push him back to earth. Caught between two opposing forces he got stuck in the middle, neither heaven nor earth. This represents the spiritually midway position. Neither here nor there.

Call it mythology or philosophy, it endeavours to provide certain answers to those questions where science still lacks clarity. There are people who believe in scientific optimism, that someday science will provide all the answers. Your 'hi' to moon reaches it in 1.2 seconds. So, you might as well agree with Haeckel that it is not worthwhile to make efforts to find out a 'thing in itself' the noumenal of Kant, when we are not even sure that it exists or not. Let everything proceed from law of substance, accept it, believe in it and forget about the rest. It is what all of us except a minuscule minority is doing. Yet there is always an element of doubt, a feeling of inadequacy.

As a child I used to wonder as to why I can't fly like birds soaring high in the skies, yet walk, hop, and flitting from one branch of the tree to other pluck the fruits by a single jump without injuring myself. Swim on the surface of the pond, river or ocean, go and swim underwater like fish without any fear of drowning. Freedom unlimited- that's the crowning desire, which we deny ourselves, because the road to freedom is long, an arduous tortuous path. A rather difficult obstacle course where you start doubting whether you will ever reach your destination or like Trishanku hanging in midyear all the time praying for the situation to come to an end.

Nachiketa, a young aspirant asked Yama, Lord of Death and the first ancestor in Indian mythology about the path of spirituality to liberation from the cycle of birth and death and this is what the Lord said. 'Rise and wake up and find yourself a wise master. It is traversing a path which is like razor's edge, the most arduous and challenging.'

This is perhaps the reason that many never make a start, some give up in the beginning and majority of the aspirants withdraw after a while. It is only a few hard-core aspirants with an immeasurable capacity for perseverance imbued with a sense of deep detachment to the objects of the world which reach the stage of enlightenment. It is said that during the last stages before enlightenment Lord Buddha, disillusioned frustrated, weak in body and mind was about to give up, when destiny pushed him forward and a final desperate stride took him past the goal.

Life had been termed as 'mysterium tremendum' and Indian philosophy of which Indian psychology is an inalienable part tries to dive deep in these issues.

With a puzzled expression, Anna shot a question to Rohit. How can as a rational thinking person you can believe in stories like a Trishanku hanging in mid space between earth and heaven when we are not sure about existence of heaven. Definitely, answered Rohit, not the story as such, including existence of Trishanku, but the symbolic expression of the struggle within. Objects all around attract us, we try to possess everything which we possibly can, and each possession leads to a desire to possess more, a never-ending process which never leaves us fully satisfied. With each possession there is temporary satisfaction, as with a meal once satisfies but again as the body clock ticks on, pangs of hunger reappear and the process goes on and on.

We will continue the discussion tomorrow. She agreed, but before parting she asked him as to how he landed up in this ashram and what his background had been. Apparently, Rohit seemed to be well educated, erudite, matured and balanced in his approach. Perhaps all the necessary qualifications to be a Guru of sorts.

I will let you in to my life history or rather life story, although once I asked a master the same question to which I got a rather cryptic reply that a renunciate like a wandering mendicant has no name and no place to show, it's the sky above and land below. I did not probe further but resolved that if I am ever asked that question, I will be much more positive in answering. So, you have my word for it. Before proceeding any further on issues of philosophy, psychology or ontology, I will share my story along with the story of this ashram with you.

Just a little diversion- you recounted an experience yesterday about the mesmerizing effect of the grandeur and awe of the Himalayas. After all, what are Himalayas as they appear. A rock face and consolidated soil which emerged out of sea of Tethys due to tectonic activity some forty million years back, which because of the prevalent climatic conditions is covered with snow. Why should a rock face so steep appear glorious and evoke a response from the senses. Think about it tonight and tomorrow we will discuss.

She just went around the village, visited a shop and bought a woolen cap to keep her warm at night and had a meal of rice along with kidney beans cooked in a tomato gravy at a local tea-house- Prem Singh aka Love lions recommendation.

The next day's conversation began about the ashram. We in our ashram here have been somewhat different and a little unorthodox, which to a certain extent differentiates us from a traditional monastic set up. We are neither in an ultra-conservative classical mode leaning towards spiritual chauvinism following the traditional order of the monks and ascetics who take vows of celibacy and renunciation, nor are we like the crass commercial establishment of modern times headed by self-styled Godmen cum gurus, where new age yoga spiced with spirituality is being marketed in various forms and hues. We do not hold any promises of transcendence or emancipation

Our setup consists of a group of volunteers who have chosen to pursue the spiritual path ensuring mutual understanding and co-operation in a liberal and friendly environment. Harmony rather than regimentation is the key word. We have framed certain rules after mutual agreement, and so far they have been complied with voluntarily. We believe in flexibility in a rational manner. We have been learning from our individual as well as collective experience and making changes whenever required. Secondly as a philosophy, we do not negate the work a day world. In fact, we consider ourselves very much a part of it, striving for a harmonious, peaceful society where universal love prevails.

One of the master's had proclaimed that he may not be considered as a special creature with special powers or dignities. 'I am no guru, nor are you my disciples. We both are fellow students in the halls of wisdom, trying together to make brotherly research into the great wisdom of the Rishis. At best, we are only equal and sincere seekers trying to do pilgrimage together in a spirit of loving brotherhood and friendly companionship.' We follow the dictum as such, each one of us being a researcher for self-discovery and realisation.

Most of the ancient Indian texts and scriptures, and especially those relating to yoga have been in sutras or aphorisms. A sutra is a thread and in ancient texts it symbolises a thread which strings together a whole lot of ideas. As comprehensive as possible.

All this while we have been attempting to reconcile the modern scientific research and advances in psychology with ancient wisdom.

Aurobindo, the great Indian philosopher remarked that Indian yoga, in essence a special formulation of certain great powers of nature, the child of immemorial ages, preserved by its vitality and truth into our modern times is now emerging out from the secret schools and ascetic retreats in which it had taken refuge, and is seeking it's place in the future sum of living powers and utilities.

In a highly competitive world, which is inhabited by shrewd politicians, unscrupulous businessman, and professional charlatans marketing religion and spirituality, we try to send a message that success is not a consequence of inflated egos manifested as increased self-affirmation and arrogance, but a result of participation in the avowed intentions of the nature. Let me now narrate the story of the ashram.

Chapter - 5

MADHAV

He was very cautiously walking on the narrow tortuous mountain path, accompanying his mother to the water spring nearby, which served as the source of drinking water to the household. Taps and pipelines were yet to arrive. A bit scared, yet elated to have been permitted to accompany his mother, with a feeling that he had come of age. Born five years earlier in a Brahmin family in the village of Harshil, Madhav Krishna Bhatt was enjoying his first real outing. He was considered responsible enough to walk on narrow mountain pathway in the neighboring forest. He had inherited hill legs, and there was a sure footedness in his gait. He would hold his mother's hand only when he found it difficult to negotiate the path on his own. This was also his first real exercise in self – confidence. First time, an entry into the forest area. What he had been imagining all this while, will now be experienced. However, since it was autumn time, so the path was not slippery. His mother Janki Devi had tied the water vessel with a rope on her back, so that the arms were free to hand hold the child and was carrying a walking stick to scare away the monkeys. She often felt that stick would also come handy, if god forbid, she encounters a leopard or a bear. While going to fetch water she used to chant her prayers, to ensure a safe passage, more so now that her child was around. The forest became denser after some distance. Although she had heard of it being inhabited by leopards and bears, however, while all the womenfolk who normally went in a group from the village to the spring source for drinking water, nobody ever encountered the deadlier among the wild animals. Not even pugmarks were seen. There were hoof marks of a barking deer, and their alarm calls heard occasionally was perhaps the only exposure to wildlife, yet the mother's instinct for child's protection was that prompted the chants. She had heard of a rare winter visit of the leopard to village when it grabbed one of the dogs which had strayed around. Most of the domesticated dogs were like shepherd dogs, well built with a spiked belt around their neck which would be a protective gear from the wild cats. These were the daring dogs which normally accompanied the shepherds in the neighboring villages who took their herd for grazing to the high-altitude meadows – ' bugyals in the local parlance.

His mother used to tell him stories about these pasturelands, some of which were valleys loaded with flowers, primulas dotted here and there, and flowers in full bloom in the rainy season. This also was the snow leopard country, an animal which was very elusive and preferred to roam around close to the snow line where it's prey the high-altitude mountain goat lived.

Madhav used to dream of valleys loaded of blooming flowers, lush green meadow grass, shining snow fields and the majestic mountain peaks which he would certainly like to explore once he grew up.

He had heard the stories about the abode of gods in the Himalayas. Someday he may come across one of the gods and seek a boon. He often fantasised about the gods. What did they look like? Were they like the calendar pictures, luminous shining ones wandering in the sky above, invisible or visible? What did they eat? Which language did they speak? Were they supposed to be very strong, yet kind to humans. What kind of miracles did they perform? Did they store a treasure house from which they distributed gifts to their loved ones. Finally, what was the best method to approach them and meet.

While accompanying his mother, he saw a very strange plant which had a green cobra like hood and attractive red berries on a cob below the hood. Mother warned him that none of the berries and wild mushrooms were touched because some of them were very poisonous. This plant was carnivorous, red colour attracted the insects which got trapped and were subsequently eaten by the plant. Plants could also be carnivorous was a new learning for him.

Every Sunday and other school holidays, it became a routine to go along with mother to the spring source through the forest, the patiently listening to the mother's stories about myths, animals, snakes, tree dwellers and gods. He was too young to discriminate between fact and fiction. It was one outing which he keenly looked forward to during the entire week. It was also offered as an incentive to be attentive in the classroom.

One day, he noticed a slight diversion, a narrower path which the mother said was a short cut to the spring source. 'Why don't we take the shorter path?' was the obvious question. A tantric mendicant has built his hut there and, it is said that he is quite a sorcerer and practices black magic. He is dangerous and is to be avoided. He was curious to know about the person, but the mother asked him to shut up and to never think about going in that direction. You even must stay away from his shadow which can cast a spell on you. It is said that he has ash smeared all over his body and indulges in strange kinds of unspeakable rituals. It is a total no go area for women and children. He was too young to understand these things, but villainous image painted of the stranger in the forest inculcated a sense of fear as well as wonderment. Was he someone human or more like a ghost? Well, he will discuss it with his friends and explore it on his own once he grows up.

He was trying to sum up the takeaway from his morning adventure into the world of nature. It was a fascinating Cobra Lily which fed itself on insects, plants poisonous, aromatic, medicinal, animals with a protective mechanism by way of alarm calls and the ascetic mendicant cum sorcerer. Someday he would love to become a Vaidya – medicine man, healer herbalist, an Ayurvedic doctor in more sophisticated terms, trained in the Indian indigenous health system.

He was very curious to find more about the wandering mendicant who had settled down in the forests. He could not keep the secret with him for a long time and decided to share it with close friends. His friends, some of them already knew about the forest dweller, but nobody had ever dared to visit him. There were stories galore. Some said that a wandering mendicant came from the Himalayas and settled here. He had the power to cast spells on people, especially children. Some said that a tree god had assumed a human form. He could survive on air and did not require any food. Another one said he could produce food out of nothing. Madhava was getting rather curious without arriving at a definite conclusion.

He could not withstand this suspense for long. With two of his close friends, one senior to him in age decided to visit the abode of the stranger. Pros and cons of the dangerous adventure were discussed, strategies were worked out and the D-day was a school holiday. Apparently all three gathered near the school ground to play football and after a while armed with small bamboo sticks went towards the forest. Mixed emotions of fear, courage, apprehensive they were on their way to unravel the great mystery.

A little distance away from the wooden hut, one of them started developing cold feet. What if the stranger got physical – after all they were children, will not be able to challenge him. Maybe they should have planned their small expedition with a larger number. But the problem with the larger number was that someone might spill the beans. However, once the fear had set in, the familiar forest started appearing dark and mystical and the best option was to retrace the steps and abort the mission. The pace was faster as if a shadow was following them. The moment the forest pathway ended, and the school ground was visible they all heaved a sigh of relief. 'Mission Ascetic' had to be postponed for another day, and new strategies to be worked out.

With 'Mission Mystique' put on the back burner life continued as as usual with school, football, seven tiles and gillidanda – a game with a stick and a 'gilli' a small wooden round piece with tapered ends, perhaps a rural raw version of what in course of time developed as cricket.

He instinctively was oriented towards non – violence. So, while playing with the sling shot he never targeted any bird, not even a flower. It was always a stone or bark of a tree.

Time flies. The young man after having completed his school education had come to Rishikesh looking for opportunities in the land of yoga.

In between, he had met the ascetic. It was when his uncle, a school teacher in town of Uttarkashi, a bachelor who showered all his affection on him had come to the village for an annual ritual worship of the family deity.

He being equally fond of his uncle expressed his desire to know about the stranger in the forest. The uncle assured him that he would take him to the ascetic, whom he had been meeting whenever he came to the village. It was he who helped him to set up his hutment in the forest. Lo and behold – the revelation was about be there.

Contrary to his expectations the stranger ascetic was just like a normal human being with grey flowing hair and beard and wearing very calm and serene expression on his glowing face. Madhav could sense a strange aura around his face – a reflection of years of penance.

After the normal greetings, he looked at Madhav with a loving expression and told his uncle that the child prodigy has been born to become an ascetic of sorts – a colourful one and revolutionary. 'What does that mean?' asked his uncle Govind. I have told you as I see his future and the rest only time will tell. He will make a name for himself, and his destiny lies here only. It was a brief meeting. It was perhaps the time for the ascetic to go into his meditation. Madhav came back happy at the prospect of following the spiritual path which he often thought about yet was never confident to discuss with his friends or relatives. It was not normal to be ascetic renunciate.

In Rishikesh, he found a job as a salesperson in a bookstore which was selling books on religion, philosophy and related subjects. Soon thereafter he got a secretarial assignment in an ashram – which involved looking after the ashram's book shop and accounting. He now realised that not everybody was a monk in the monastic setup. The management consisted of people who were responsible for maintenance, day to day operations, running the kitchen, and a score of other odd jobs so that the Swamis had ample time for indulgence in spiritual activities. With his temperament and simplicity, he in course of time became close to Swami Someshwaranand and started attending his discourses. Here was a lay person who was showing signs of a 'mumukshu' – an aspirant for spiritual activity.

Swami ji was a storehouse of knowledge, his domain went beyond the religious scriptures and philosophy and covered physics, life sciences, psychology, history. Where did the swami ji get the opportunity for learning a vast array of subjects? Which college or university did he go to? He was told that you should inculcate the habit of asking questions and then start looking for answers. It comes from within, provided you have a deep desire for it. Once the Guru inside you gets propitiated then rest follows, because you become your own mentor, guide and teacher. Each morning a new vista opens, a new potential actualizes.

Next week onwards there was going to be a series of discourses on Yoga and meditation, which Madhav was keenly looking forward to.

However, Swamiji was in a mood to talk. He informally initiated him into the basics of Vedanta. During the discourses he became aware that attainment of perfection is the conscious integration of Being. Intuitional Revelation is the method. Intuition is an integral experience, which apprises you with degrees of imperfection, and of intellectual experience of infinite being. It is not by mere metaphysical speculation, intellectual ratiocination that Being can be understood. It is a non-relational experience, wherein the distinction between experiencing subject and experienced object gets obliterated. Being enters into Being.

Truth the true content in a 'golden vessel' is covered by multiple psychic layers. These are the obstacles which need to be negotiated with extreme caution.

Truth is perennial existence, limitless awareness and limitless joy. Upanishads outline the Transcendental Mysticism – not an effect of emotional outburst, but a transcendence of intellect and reason into an arena of higher intuitive wisdom.

Stronger the ego, more is the weight on your back, greater the harmony stronger is the social bond as well as compliance with the spiritual law. Yoga is primarily ego shedding. It is an ever-expanding universe from a relative point of view. Since the Universe is expanding and therefore changing every moment, change is the law of life. A felt necessity for a fuller state of experience is the mother of all attraction and repulsions.

It is a journey where you move from a transitory lower existent to eternal higher existent.

State of Perfection is neither an indivisibility nor a manifest multiplicity. It is something indescribable, ineffable.

Too dense or terse for a novitiate. He requested Swamiji to explain in somewhat simpler terms, to which his answer was that just try to think over every word I have spoken over the next week and we will discuss.

The discussion never took place, because destiny was to take a new turn. His forays into the forest inculcated the spirit of pursuit of knowledge, esoteric as well as exoteric. As providence would have it, his childhood dream was to come true, when he got admission for a course in Ayurveda in the Gurukul Kangri, an old institution of learning in the neighboring town of Haridwar.

His career had taken a new turn. Ayurveda- the science of life was termed as upveda or a subsidiary text of Atharvaveda- a science of health and healing. It was about balancing the three humors in the human body. Vaat, the air principle, Pitta the fire principle and Cough the water principle. There were interesting texts like Charak Samhita and Sushruta Samhita which laid emphasis on a healthy lifestyle by way of proper diet. In Ayurveda the measure of your health was not what you eat but how well you digest the food. These were very elaborate texts about right life style, right diet, seasonal changes, healing herbs and included surgery.

One of the cardinal principles of Ayurveda was about truthfulness and honesty, which was stated in a verse, which said that a dishonest Vaidya was worse than Yamaraja- the lord of death. Yamaraja only took your life whereas a dishonest doctor took your money as well as your life. It inculcated in him a very strong sense of truthfulness and integrity. Fortified with a degree in Ayurvedic medicinal system he returned back to the ashram and had become one of the most popular and competent yoga instructors. He also understood the close linkage between Ayurveda and Yoga – a very strong wellness regime.

Chapter - 6

VERONICA

Then came Veronica on the scene. Young, extremely intelligent and ambitious, smart, beautiful, sexy and vivacious, who was ever willing to manipulate her tricks and techniques to achieve her ends. The enchanting temptress was temperamentally just the opposite to what yoga philosophy stood for. Every other person for her was a means to an end- the fulfilment of her unending desires.

Her 'Mission India' was 'Operation Poaching'. She had been running a wellness retreat in a village called Vinci near Florence in Italy. Yoga was the latest addition to the wellness regime. Most of so-called new age Godmen, who had acquired a celebrity status were heading towards America, land of dreams where they could make their millions. Europe still had a lot of unexplored fertile areas. She was looking for someone who could play second fiddle to her.

Ethics and morals did not figure in her scheme of things. It was success, the end product which mattered. She was willing to pay the price if it made commercial sense. For her everybody had a price, whether in money terms or otherwise. Sophisticated sexual seductress had too many weapons in her armory to knock out whomsoever she wanted to within a short time. Her keen discerning eye had already spotted the target, the handsome young Himalayan highlander, who had been born and brought up in the lap of nature and his face glowed with a childlike innocence. It had not yet been corrupted by the ways of the wicked world. Her methods were very subtle and sophisticated. By now she had learnt stories from the Indian mythology where the king of heaven Indra felt threatened by the ascetic, he sent the celestial dancers to lure them. The task was for this beautiful earthly dame to lure away the ascetic in the making.

Next to hunger, sex is supposed to be the most powerful instinct. It has to be presented in the most subtle manner for weaning away the young ascetic by painting an alluring picture of greener pastures of Europe. He was the best among the yoga instructors, both physically and temperamentally. The body was flexible and supple as if it had no bones. Temperamentally, here was a youngster with tremendous patience and fortitude. Not yet into an ultra-conservative mode as some of his older colleagues were. How far is his moral and ethical dilemma going to be a hurdle, she was yet to assess. Without any formal degree in psychology, she had an instinctive uncanny sense by which she could judge people and build relationships accordingly. The discerning eye was her great asset. She found Madhav to be quite different from day one. He was yet to decide about his final destination and yet was not overpowered or overawed by the monastic discipline. He was very positive about life and yoga, yet not prima facie averse to the contrary views. She soon realised that neither the sexual seductress nor the alluring temptress would succeed with him. His ambitions went beyond the lure of lucre or pleasures of bed. He could only be lured by an ideal which will appeal to him by putting him on high moral ground.

The strategy had to be very different, and she was in no hurry. Madhav, s upbringing in verdant himalayan valley and resulting simplicity and innocence were his prime assets, his USP, and she had to work on that. She had to foster in him a missionary zeal, where locations did not matter. He could be the harbinger of neo spirituality to Europe. A genuine natural romantic, liberal and catholic in his approach. She had to convince him that there are more things on this earth and heaven that we ever dream of and a bit of adventure will always do him some good.

She had always been proud of her manipulative skills. Selfishness, it is said is an innate trait of humans, but the degrees vary. It is a survival instinct, but if it is tempered by selflessness it makes you more courageous and entitled to better outcomes. However, till now her measure of morality was success. She never bothered about the sense of guilt coupled with stark selfishness. It was always brushed under the carpet and consigned to the subconscious.

Yet one factor she had not bargained for. If she could influence others by her behaviour, she would be equally vulnerable. It's a two-way relationship. The peace and serenity prevailing in the monastic setup was influencing her both at conscious and subconscious levels.

All along she had been strategising to befriend the target, build a relationship which would make the target more vulnerable.

In Indian culture and philosophy there is a concept of 'Satsang', company of good, intelligent and truthful people and beneficial influence it has on an individual. She was perhaps mistaken in her assessment in the sense that simple truthful people were more vulnerable. In fact, it was otherwise. They were much more rational and less gullible, because they do not suffer from strange complexes and their desires and ambitions were limited.

Only time was going to tell how things were going to work out. In the initial interactions with him, she started arguing in favour of neo spirituality to which his stance was quite different. When you pursue the spiritual path as an aspirant, the ultimate goal is transcendence, so spirituality is beyond the time dimension. Classical, ancient, modern or neo spirituality are only expressions from a practical point of view.

Madhav who was yet to take his vows of celibacy and cutting off social relationship by Viraj ritual was not averse to exploring the world and exposure to new ideas. He was a man of the modern times and had every right to know about the societal changes, emerging philosophies, different lifestyles, cultural patterns, scientific advancement and prevalent civilisational trends.

Veronica was on cloud nine for a while, when he consented to accompany her to Vinci, land of Mona Lisa's creator.

Madhav was a bit apprehensive, yet quite excited. He had not yet committed himself to a life of a renunciate in a monastic setup. With the added degree of an Ayurvedic doctor, he will postpone his decision. Here was an opportunity, not only to promote Yoga but Ayurveda as well. Life science pushed to the back burner due to circumstances. A holistic system of medicine in dire need of research and integration with other prevalent systems of health and medicine.

Chapter - 7

MADHAV AT VINCI

It was a group of ski enthusiasts who were on their way back from Abetone in Tuscany and had checked in at the luxury resort for rest and rejuvenation. The Yoga package was part of the wellness regime.

Madhav was introducing Yoga exercises to the group highlighting the difference between Yoga postures and breathing, and the conventional physical exercises. While the sympathetic nervous system representing fight or flight syndrome response along with the cortical regions of the brain dominated the conventional exercises, it was the para sympathetic nervous system representing rest and relax along with sub cortical regions of the brain were dominant in Yoga. Conventional physical exercise led to increased muscle tension along with forceful rapid movements. Yoga was about slow dynamic and static movements, micro stresses in the muscle along with controlled and natural breathing in a relaxed manner, energising the body. Yoga postures are part of a psycho physical cum spiritual activity.

In Yoga the focus was internally oriented, while in other exercises the focus was on the externals. Burning calories was more important in conventional exercises whereas Yoga is based on the principle of conservation of energy.

Yoga is a game of harmony not for those who are either overindulgent in sensory pleasure or the extremely austere ones. It is not about the mortification of the body. Moderation, balance and harmony are keywords.

Angelina, angel faced young lady wanted to know if Madhav could initiate her into meditation. "No way" replied Madhav, abruptly to the extent of sounding rude. Angelina's face, fell. Madhav sensing her facial expression felt bad and somewhat apologetically said "I myself have been grappling all these years with preliminary activities and don't find myself competent to teach others.

"Why so many of your Godmen from India in the past have claimed to initiate people into it."

I would love to satisfy your curiosity and remove the doubts once this session is over. They decided to meet in the evening before dinner.

Responding to her question he said "Firstly, the word Godmen does not find a place in the lexicon of Yoga. All aspiring yogis are humans, some slightly more evolved due to years of practice. Yoga is a godwards journey and therefore the myth of Godmen needs to be shattered.

Yoga is a discipline which has either been over emphasised or under stated, sometimes misconstrued, often deliberately misrepresented by the self-styled masters, gurus, non gurus and so called gurus of various hues with an agenda of their own.

It was a kind of discourse which she was listening to with rapt attention.

"One of the great masters said that the great adventure of yoga is not easy for those people whose mind is distracted by various occupations. The problem is the human mind. It considers itself as sovereign while it is limited, fickle to the extent that it cannot entertain more than a single thought at a time. It has a very limited spectrum. It just cannot decipher any unfamiliar language.

Monkeys like it jump from one tree to another. Movement is it's characteristic and favourite pastime- undisciplined, always in disorder."

Perhaps it's polygamous nature is due to its presiding deity- the moon. Moon according to Indian mythology had twenty-seven wives, all daughters of King Daksha. The wives were the nakshatras, the lunar mansions. He was partial to one wife called Rohini to the consternation of others. Rest of them complained to their father who cursed moon to become a leper. However, the curse was diluted by the great God Shiva-the auspicious one, whereby it waxed and waned during the luminous and dark fortnights. So, first of all flirting mind has to be reined in. Purifying it is the first prerequisite for meditation. Meditation with an impure and impulsive mind will cause more harm than any benefit.

In Royal yoga, there are six limbs for self-purification, sense control and mind control before meditation. It is the ultimate stage of yoga. The final stage after this is Samadhi the communion with God or salvation. It calls for total purity and integrity of mind apart from great tenacity and highest effort, deepest possible aspiration for perfection. It involves uniting reason with feeling. It is the science of the Absolute. The toughest part is that ego sense or individuality has to be gradually diluted to the extent that it ultimately disappears.

Herculean task indeed! So, in a practical life practising a bit of mindfulness and relaxation by way of Yoga nidra or Yogic sleep is a betteroption,, practical and beneficial. We are different from the animals because of a mind that reasons. In Yoga it is a qualitative transformation from humans to the divine level, where soul or spirit comes into operation. That is why I confessed my inability to initiate you to the process. You just cannot evolve from a human to divine in a matter of few days. It's the truth which may sound unpleasant but is a reality. That's why Indian scriptures say it is like walking on a razors edge, where all your skills and determination are put to a very severe test.

Concentration precedes meditation. It involves disciplining the mind which armed with its strong ego sense and sensory aids is ever willing to rise in revolt. It will ask all the sleeping dogs lying within to wake up and join it. It has innumerable neurons firing, millions of thoughts hiding within it. Someone used to changing his attire every moment does not yield to surrender it's liberty to get into a uniform. The carrot of elevation of it's status has to dangled before it, convince it and gradually upgrade it by a process of sublimation. If we are able to make it smell the fragrance of divinity the transformation starts. The nature of mind is averse to concentration. It has to be convinced that by a gradual surrender of authority will result in an ultimate gain.

The days dialogue left him thinking whether in Patanjali bashing he had gone too far or in a modern world view we have to take recourse to more practical solutions to our problems. A missionary zeal to spread a philosophy in an honest way casts a big responsibility on the Guru to reveal all aspects, good bad and indifferent, without any subjective bias. The mission was to spread the idea of nonviolence, love and compassion. The methodology came afterwards.

He was being honest when he said that meditation as enunciated by Patanjali was not easy to practice. He thought of the master who had said that meditation is an activity of the soul and not of body and mind and therefore the path is full of obstacles. His Italian sojourn in Tuscany region had provided him an opportunity to read and discuss Dante,s Divine Comedy. Paradiso could only be reached after going through Inferno the hell and Purgatory, the place for repentance. Dante had Virgil as guide in Inferno and so were St. Beatrice and others. So you had the most competent, experienced gurus to guide you to Paradise. Can you find a Guru of that calibre in the modern era? He perhaps will have to shape his own world view somewhat differently. All life after all is a great learning experience and it is not constrained by the time factor. Back to the Masters views which described meditation as a process of internalising the externals and then go on to universalise it. A state of thoughtlessness, where the awareness that I am meditating should also disappear. It is an ideal state where the self or the soul has realised itself. Mind being rid of it's wanderlust the self gets established in itself, the ideal state of existence consciousness and infinite bliss, God so as to say. According to the Master it is very rare that soul acts in day to day life, but when it acts in a very mild or distorted way then it results in extreme pleasure, where a person becomes oblivious of the world around. In normal life it gets reflected in satisfaction of intense hunger, sexual appetite and deep sleep. Even in a distorted form it is a release of tension although temporarily. Patanjali talks of obstacles and hurdles on the Godwards path of yoga. The major nine obstacles are illness, physical or mental, inertia and laziness, sensual craving, doubt, false perception, inability to attain higher state of consciousness and having attained it to continue living in it. These hurdles are not supposed to be insurmountable but call for extreme effort, perseverance, patience coupled with a deep sense of detachment. Theoretically possible but practically almost impossible. Dante also talks of nine concentric circles in Inferno the hell, where you are punished according to the gravity of your sins. Violence fraud and treachery involve worst torture.

The path to freedom of Paradise is paved with thorns. It can be travelled only by pure souls. In Hathayoga it is symbolised by the rise of serpent power ascending through various Chakras, centres or knots of whirling life energy. Master says that among the evolved aspiring yogis they only go up to the second or third chakra, thereby depicting our vulnerability while walking on the razors edge.

He felt a little confused. All this while he had been very confident about his knowledge of yoga and speaking authoritatively. He took every word of the classical texts for granted except once in a while, when studying Ayurveda looking for linkages between various systems of medicine and therapy, holistic concepts, and it's scientific interpretation. He often wondered that most of the texts of Ayurveda as well as Yoga were of a different era and to an extent culture specific. He always felt the need for updating it, and integrating it with changing times. With an European experience rich in modern medicine and psychology, whether it was time to go back to India and get involved in some inclusive research in Yoga incorporating its physical, mental and spiritual aspects. A visit to Abetone and it's botanical park with fir trees made him extremely nostalgic. For a moment he wondered as to how Harshil had changed so much. Where had the ever effusive Bhagirathi disappeared.? A few days later while reading the Divine comedy the desire to go back to the roots became much stronger reading the lines:

By now the sun was crossing the meridian of the horizon whose highest point covers Jerusalem, and from Ganges, night circling opposite the sun was moving together with the scales that, when the length of dark defeats the day, desert night's hands.

How could he stay away from Ganges and the Himalayas for ever. The call of the river was beckoning him to the path of return.

Chapter - 8

MADHAV ON YOGA

If you view the whole gamut of Patanjali,s yoga it is deep philosophy and psychology, but how many of us really aspire for salvation? All we want is a happy healthy and prosperous life, comfortable without any major problems. Minor issues we feel we can always handle. We want to be endowed with strength, power courage and all the wherewithal for as comfortable and healthy life as it can be in the best possible friendly environment. Security from womb to tomb, with a little bit of adventure here and there. Pleasure interspersed with adventure, excitement and wellness is what we pursue. All worshipping, liturgy, seeking blessings of God is to that end. We want philosophy to cater to our practical needs in life. We seldom think of afterlife and that too in a rather casual manner. Yoga of meditation therefore becomes the most difficult proposition in work a day life. One of the masters has said that almost all institutions including those of yoga have a social environment where it is near impossible for a person to isolate himself and be a true renunciate.

No wonder less rigorous and relatively simpler techniques of yoga emerged which could easily be reconciled with the day to day life of a householder.

Starting with idea of mindfulness by way of anapansati and vipassana there emerged Hathayoga which promises good health mental relaxation and a friendly disposition towards everyone around.

While various schools of Buddhism also laid emphasis on meditation starting with mindfulness, the liberal and less orthodox school know as Mahayana the great path also accepted the tantra practices without it's sexual overtones and the new practical approach diluted moral codes, ethical observances and rigorous self control, and started with purificatory exercises laying emphasis on the body. Body purification is where we start with and maybe subsequently try to train the mind. The emphasis is on the body. So purification of bodily organs, energy channels called nadis- the Yogic neural system, right functioning of endocrinal system by way of Asana and Pranayama gets a priority. A pure and healthy body then becomes fit for meditation for those who choose the path. It offers more flexibility compared to the relative rigidity of Raj yoga. It is this genre, this methodology which has become popular because of a pragmatic approach. This is where the captains of sunrise yoga industry saw the potential of commercial exploitation to establish themselves with money and power by way of commodification of a spiritual concept.

"We start our chanting with Om. What's the significance of it?" asked Angelina. Let me clarify. It's not a mere word or sound. It is the great symbol of God. It is supposed to be a primal vibration- pranava mantra, a divine chant which induces life in everything. It is the primal vibration, the singularity of big bang- creatrix of everything we come across in this universe. It is the energy or force of pure consciousness. Whenever we chant Aum we do not make a sound from our body, but generate an energy within which is our real personality. Chant of Aum is like a wave thinking the ocean. We identify ourselves with the energy of the universe and merge into it. It is an impersonal universal vibration. It is the symbol of total inclusivity.

He introduced Krishnamacharya, to whom the modern generation owed a lot, because majority of the asanas were developed by him. But along with his mention came the realisation that among the visitors while many of them evinced an interest in Yoga there were very few takers for Ayurveda. Some showed more of an academic interest rather than taking it seriously. Herbal concoctions were looked more as a novelty rather than an essential element of alternative therapy. Yoga had been popular in the West, whereas people were totally unaware of Indian system of medicine. He had taken up the Ayurveda course inspired by Krishnamacharya who combined yoga with Ayurveda. He seriously felt that it was time to go back before he forgets all that he had learned about Ayurveda. His aide Anand with a recognised yoga degree had been assisting him for last two years. His absence was not going to leave a void. Veronica by this time had established her resorts brand equity in Yoga and wellness and he was going to leave behind a worthy successor.

Chapter - 9

MADHAV RETURNS

Having spent five years in Italy and equipped with an European experience, Madhav realised that it had been a great learning experience. It had been a wonderful exposure to new ideas, a different culture, an altogether different life style. A totally different socio cultural environment, impressive in certain respects. The basic necessities of life like food shelter and clothing taken care of.

There were lessons to be learnt from Renaissance. Italian art and architecture,design, German engineering, French cuisine. Alps and Mediterranean were finding a way into his ever expanding horizon of experience. Different philosophies, different thoughts, an altogether different orientation of the mind towards a material outlook towards relationships, new definitions regarding social and individual behaviour were cropping up with each new visitor to the resort. There were people to whom yoga and wellness mattered. There were others who thought of it as a big hoax, and were least interested in it. Nobody seemed to be keenly interested in the philosophies of the orient. There were times when he thought that East is east and West is westand never the twain shall meet. However there were few of the visitors who felt that following a simple yoga exercise regime and bit of mindfulness would help them lead a better life. There were mixed responses and reactions. Those who made an effort to come to India to an ashram had a much keener interest in undergoing a new novel experience. This set him thinking whether to stay back or go back to the roots and look for a future there.

"You seem to be very unique specimen among the human resource professionals, effective yet someone apparently seeming to be withdrawn. You seem to have mastered the art of creating a strange utopian environment, a make believe world of oriental imagination, creative flair wherein you try to infuse God in us. Brilliant, absolutely brilliant." Madhav could sense the sarcasm, a sense of jealousy borne out of ignorance, sense of superiority smacking of white man's burden. Perhaps it was time to go back and try to attract more understanding and interested audiences. It was time to revisit the whole gamut of yoga as a human resource development for establishing a better society professing the principles of truth, justice, non violence and love. Harmony all around. New age yoga addressing the concerns of baby boomers and generation X has to be developed. What a learning experience it had been for young highlander from the himalayas carrying the baggage of orthodoxy, conservatism, and a sense of morality which left little room for any innovation.

Chapter - 10

TRIPATHA ASHRAM

Madhav‚s presence in Veronica's resort proved to be a game changer. It was his sincerity, integrality and honesty along with his knowledge of Yoga led to creation of the brand equity of the retreat. He had become a great influencer. While Veronica made her millions for which she felt obliged to this strange influencer, she had also become his admirer. Over a five year period the relationship had a healthy growth, both happy and satisfied. She, because her business had greatly expanded and the footfall at her place was much beyond her expectations and he because of an altogether different exposure, new ideas and a new learning.

When he expressed his desire to go back and set up an ashram at Harshil, she told him that she was more than willing to invest in it without expecting any returns in monetary terms, but would love to share the results of any research. It was more of a philanthropic gesture on behalf of a rich and successful business woman. The redeeming influence of a noble and pious soul. Madhav had an able successor in Ananda who like Madhav had a degree in Ayurveda and a diploma in Yoga, and almost ten years of working experience. Ananda was a talented young person, soft spoken always keen to enhance his skills. Madhav 's savings along with the Veronica's financial help, he had to work out the framework of a modern research oriented ashram where the tradition blended with modernity, a knowledge hub which would keep alive the spirit of Yoga and Vedanta and incorporate the new discoveries of science and advances in psychology. It was not only Veronica, but few of her rich guests who had been influenced by him also wanted to chip in. There are times when some people felt that it was like funding a research project for public welfare. While the government as well as the corporates or venture capitalists funded research projects where there were possibilities of high returns and financial gains, in this hitherto unexplored area which is likely to lead to new possibilities in wellness sector. Was it charity, philanthropy or a long term planning.

The Ashram would do away with certain rigidities of rituals and would be progressive rather than conservative in accepting positive changes in thought. It was conceived on a quasi monastic mode where voluntarily compliance with the ashram's rules and management principles would be encouraged, and norms be laid down with consensus by the permanent inmates. The rituals like Viraj Yagya and Atma Shraddha for initiation in sanyasa were to be done away with.

What are those rituals? queried Anna.

Viraj Yagya was a sacrificial ritual where a person decides to abstain from rajas or all movement, namely worldly affairs, thereby severing all relationships with people, and performing one's own post funerary rites because of cutting off all relationships with people who otherwise would have performed your Shraddha.

It involved fasting for a day, waking up the whole night performing a vigil, asserting your determination to follow the path of renunciation. One categorical imperative was about Ahimsa or non violence implying a vegetarian meal and non injury principle to the extent it was practical. It automatically implied the message of love and compassion for all persons and objects.

Dreaming about his project on his Lufthansa flight to Delhi, he thought of an advertisement about the airlines, which said that Lufthansa is different because of it's unique hospitality, comfort, and service, his project is going to be different. It is going to be imbued with philanthropic principles of love, welfare and wellness backed by traditional knowledge as well as modern trends, with adequate **orientation towards** spirituality. Instead of spiritual chauvinism it was going to be spirituality moderated to life's practical needs factoring in the prevalent socio cultural environment.

After having spent a few days in Delhi and Rishikesh, Madhav finally landed in Harshil to the delight of the local village folks. Madhav's ancestral property was to be converted into the Ashram. The entire village was very enthusiastic about it and everyone was willing to contribute in cash or kind. With the blessing of all mighty, grace of God and participation of friends and well wishers the Ashram was established. As I had told you earlier that it was Madhav,s vision which made us somewhat unorthodox. Now I am going to narrate my life story.

Chapter - 11

KALEIDOSCOPE

As a child amongst my most cherished memories vivid till date, was of visiting the local fair along with my mother. Just close to the end of the rainy season and advent of autumn in terms of lunar months, the fair was held. Idols of a local mountain deity sculpted from local material like banana stem, were temporarily erected on a make shift stage after a consecration ceremony were finally consigned to the holy waters of a river after the fair was over. My mother, pious in her intentions, religious in her orientation, went every year to pay her obeisance to the deity, a routine which was scrupulously followed till her death.

For me oblivious of the religious significance, the fair provided me an opportunity to gather toys of my choice. What fascinated me the most was a crude locally assembled kaleidoscope where in were innumerable colourful patterns.

A slight tilt either to left or right the pattern changed. Delighted I was to be the possessor of a magical instrument like that. What made me restless was that my child mind was not able to understand the principle of magic involved. None of my neighbourhood friends of my age, whom I could trust were able to explain the phenomenon. I decided to approach the shopkeeper, who endowed with the right mentality of a trader agreed to explain it provided I bought another piece. Already possessing one, I dare not ask my mother for another piece for fear of being reprimanded and mentally cursed the selfish shopkeeper no end, with whatever curse words were there etched in my child memory. No easy solution appeared, without weighting the pros and cons, I took the risk and with a brave action on my part. I disassembled the toy in my possession. To my utter surprise and disappointment what constituted the apparently magical toy of mine were a few mirrors joined in a triangular shape along with a few pieces of coloured glass bangles. In a moment, the magic had disappeared and gone were the multiple colourful patterns. All my attempts thereafter to reassemble and restore the magic were unsuccessful. Perhaps my only option was to write the obituary of the toy.

I suddenly remembered the temple priest telling my mother that the idol after consecration by way of right rituals becomes a powerful deity, worshipping which grants desired results in terms of worldly possessions.

Thereafter began my quest for the right rituals of consecration to restore the magical powers of my toy. I realized that expecting any response from a deity, some offerings had to be made, the right gift of the right nature. Looking for a gift hurriedly went through my mother's small bamboo basket which she invariably carried to the temple. Further disappointment was in store for me. All it contained was a few withered flowers, cotton wicks, incense sticks, match box and a small container of clarified butter. Nothing worthwhile except for a small prayer book which was beyond my comprehension.

After recurrent failure with the group of friends and with my limited resources, I thought of consulting one of the sadhus -half clad ash smeared wandering mendicants who along with a begging bowl to collect the alms seemed to appear from nowhere at the beginning of the fair and competed with the lepers, handicapped persons and the less privileged persons for a share of the limited beggars space.

What differentiated them from others was their arrogant attitude, which was enough to scare a child like me. Added to that were the stories of ghosts and spirits that associated with their strange and mysterious rituals.

With various options ruled out the head not responding to any possible solution, the heart put forward the option of approaching one of the parents. After all, blood is thicker than water. The very thought of grim profile of the father to such a question discouraged unnecessary queries that end. Then suddenly a thought flashed. The priest telling my mother once that secret knowledge about things religious was their exclusive preserve. However, to share any part of this knowledge he had to be compensated either in cash or kind. Dakshina – fees by way of offering for services rendered. Since they claimed to be the intermediaries between the gods and lesser humans, they being in an exalted position looked for opportunities and preferred a recurring income option to one time compensation. Either I could become an understudy to one of them or wait to grow up into an understanding adult.

The simple problem of patterns of the Kaleidoscope had assumed complex proportions and I had no answers for it. Later on when I climbed up the ladder in terms of a promotion to a higher class in school after successfully clearing the obstacle called examinations. which a genius like Einstein termed as a nightmare because it tested your scholarly proclivities, knowledge, capacity, competence and intelligence put together in a limited time irrespective of your physical or psychological condition. No wonder the system flawed from beginning did not exist in India in ancient times in Gurukul tradition and most of the progressive educational systems modified their learning procedures by lessening the shock of examinations by replacing it with continuous assessment. However, I wasn't lucky that way, but I realizing to my satisfaction that the problems of physics have been investigated right from the day the stars, planets, sun and moon fascinated us, regulated our life according to their position. Astrology and astronomy had sown the seeds of future physics.

It was too early in life to think about complex metaphysical issues, simple arithmetic problems had easy determinate solutions. One plus one made two, whether you were in North Pole or South Pole. Gravity had no impact on the numbers. Mathematics represented a logical sequence, an empirical unity of perception, except in certain cases where things tended to zero or infinity which upset the apple cart forcing you to approximate solutions, often leaving a grey area. Later I realized, it was no wonder that Idealist Kant as well as Dualist Descartes, both heralding a revolution in Western philosophy, could not abandon their love for mathematics.

While the mystery of the toy kaleidoscope was unravelled by as illusion created by conjoined mirrors effecting multiple reflections, beautiful patterns emerging out of broken and divided pieces of coloured glass, it was not so simple to explain the principles of Kaleidoscopic Universe, illusion as an appearance or reality encountered each day in life.

While we assume all objects to be static, universe is actually just a movement conditioned by space time changing every moment. The fluid ever expanding universe is an organic living whole where God and Brute crossed each other's path at some point.

Before moving on to the problems of the wider kaleidoscope there are some very mundane things about my life, which I feel unimportant.

Chapter - 12

WIDER KALEIDOSCOPE

In the characteristic style of an Indian cab driver who in order to earn some merit always believed in the theory of instilling fear of God on the helpless passengers, swerved the vehicle suddenly to the left, applied the brakes and the vehicle came to a screeching halt near the pump in the filling station to take fuel for the onwards journey. The station was located a few miles short of Rishikesh, the 'Yoga capital of the World'. However, to atone for his somewhat atrocious behaviour, the cab driver had the sincerity to tell the passengers that next to the petrol pump was also the last filling station for spirits, and thereafter it was miles of prohibition ahead. Further there was no scope for any kind of meat dishes being served at Rishikesh, nor was there any availability of processed non-vegetarians foods like cold cuts or canned tuna and sardines. The food stall Dhaba in the local parlance was next to the liquor shop and the two following the Yoga principle were in close harmonious co-ordination with each other.

For a moment I thought about the behaviour of the taxi driver. We had started early morning for Delhi, co – passengers being picked up from different locations and he had been very steady at the wheel.

Once in a while lamenting about the pot holes, unruly traffic, the bullock carts laden with sugarcane, the odd cyclist or a three wheeler defying all rules of traffics, driving through the city with multiple speed breakers, and traffic delays due to traffic jams. An average cab – driver who did not own the vehicle lead a very wretched life. There were no fixed duty hours Reporting from 1 a.m. in the morning to 12 at night to suit the convenience of the passengers, inspite of lack of sleep had to be steady on the wheel. Had to contend with unruly traffic, pot holed undulating road surface, road rage, and enforcement authorities including police whose palms always lacked grease. His behaviour was to be immaculate with the passengers, however, unreasonable they may be, because that affected his tip. They were paid very low wages by the vehicle owners on the pretext that they earned handsome tips. Most of the time he was eating at roadside eateries and home food was more of a delicacy, a privilege once in a while. All these frustrations were taken out on the helpless vehicle yet ensuring that there was no ostensible damage, which he may have to compensate.

However, coming to food, the very sight of artificially coloured lifeless chicken hanging on the skewers awaiting their turn for final roasting in the clay oven called Tandoor was not at all appetising, so I decided albeit temporarily in favour of vegetarianism.

Meanwhile, I enquired from the cab driver about the risk involved in carrying liquor to the prohibited territory ahead. In his own characteristic style he tried to convince me that life in this world does not offer any risk free experience. Life is primarily about discounting the risk factor by your own ingenuity. From the moment of your birth when you take the first deep breath, you enter the risk laden world, constantly challenged by it, and learning to skirt it by application of your instinct and mind. Humans, he said philosophically have been endowed with a developed mind for this purpose only. In the unlikely event of your being caught with the prohibited stuff a policy of appeasement by shelling out a few bucks to the inspecting authorities ensured a safe passage. Here was my first lesson on Yoga on my way to the capital that life is primarily about harmony with fellow beings and prevalent environment and key to subjective and objective satisfaction lay in appeasement and compromises by ego-shedding.

However, coming from a conservative Brahmin family, following the traditions of lineage society where family prestige enunciated as Kul Dharma was very important, I finally could not bring myself to flout the excise law because risk averse behaviour was perhaps not there in my sanskar. For me, between the three major Indian goddess the balance always titled towards Saraswati, the goddess of learning knowledge and wisdom rather than Laxmi symbolising prosperity and opulence and Kali the destroyer of evil. Inspired by the drivers skill who had quite successfully managed to weave his way through patches of road where pot holes dominated the scenario, multiple diversions through countryside with roughest possible road surface, my faith in the indigenous crisis management system called 'Jugad'got further strengthened. The first principle of the 'Jugad' system of management, (incidentally what they don't teach you in business schools) was that everything can be managed somehow other, and this 'somehow and other' had an almost illimitable undefined domain. It was left to your talent, manipulative skills and competence to find solutions to all kinds of problems, simple, complex, extreme in face of all adversities.

After weighting the risk factors involved, I postponed my decision to buy liquor for the time being and hoping to explore safer and less riskier opportunities at the destination.

Moving a little further, I felt a little encouraged by a signage on the roadside which read 'you are now entering the abode of gods, welcome to the Yoga capital'. The very mention of land of gods brought back the childhood stories of heaven and hell. The gods were propitiated to earn merit for an entry to the heavens, which offered flowing rivers of nectar, celestial singers and dancers, damsels extremely beautiful, whereas in hell you were like the chicken on skewers to be fried in hot oil, a place of constant unending torture. While heaven was ruled by gods in hell the demons were the masters.

Liquor being out of mind for a while, pondering about heaven and hell, gods and humans, merit and sin I entered our destination Rishikesh. However, we were told by the discerning ones that the original name of the place was Hrishikesh which over a period of time got corrupted to Rishikesh. While Hrishikesh conveyed 'Lord of the sense' a name by which Lord Krishna the god incarnate was also addressed and Rishikesh meant hair of a sage. Since both the names had somewhat sacred overtones, Rishikesh being easier on the tongue, I decided to accept it as such.

Further the valley nestled in the lower Himalayas was a region where Lord Shiva, the Adiyogi – the first divine proponent of Yoga prevailed because of being a denizen of Himalayan region and had as his consort the daughter of the great Himalayan mountain in mythological tradition.

Itihasa Purana – a combination of history and ancient tradition, mythology carried forward by folk lore, the territories had been carved out where personal anthropomorphic gods ruled. While legend of Lord Ram, Maryada Purushottam, the ideal personality the supreme person full of honour and righteousness, hero of epic ' Ramayana' – dominated the central and eastern part of province ofU.P., Lord Krishna the Lord incarnate endowed with sixteen divine arts or propensities like compassion, patience justice, beauty, truth etc. and controller of senses legend originating in Mathura and Vrindavan prevailed in the Western part of the country. Himalayan region apart from being abode of gods was also the land of Shiva who initially danced into the Hindu pantheon with his Tandava, the cosmic dance of creative destruction established a pan-Indian presence. Here was the original fertility god, the god of the farmers, the terrible Rudra of the Vedas combined with Agni and Indra, the first Yogi, the first dancer, an ash smeared ascetic., God of the poor could easily be propitiated by a simple offering of water on the ling –the visible symbol of the invisible power of all inclusive Absolute.

Here was the fascinating five faced god, acting in eight modes, creator, sustainer destroyer all in one.

I suddenly became aware that the hierarchy and the protocol among the Lords divine also changed region wise. It was a kind of 'deitistic parochialism' which explained their dominance over a region. Perhaps the local gods were psychologically nearer to the inhabitants of the area therefore easier to identify with and could easily be super imposed with local custom, culture and traditions.

I finally checked in at a local lodge which suited my pocket and thought process shifted from divine to more mundane matters.

Immediate problem at hand was to harmonise consumption of spirit with spirituality in the land of Yoga. To my utter consternation I had discovered that perhaps under the influence of religious leaders the political leaders decided that spirituality prohibited consumption of spirituous liquor. I thought of Vedic gods, especially Indra, the king of gods, a warrior fond of soma – the Vedic brew and perhaps was the Indian counterpart of Bacchus and Dionysus. According to mythology he was accused of patricide, killing his father Tvashtra in a fight over soma liquor. I was given to understand that there were no temples of Bhairava also where traditional offerings were liquor. However smoking of marijuana as an escape route went well in propitiating Lord Shiva with a chant of 'Jai Shambhu', a few drags of the hemp grass elevated you in the path of realisation of the invisible spirit, while the visible liquid form was considered a poor depressing anti dote.

The intoxicants also vied with each other for their status in the hierarchy, spirituous liquor eventually lost out in the land of gods, because of its presumptive association with the demons.

Finally, I decided in favour of a pure vegetarian meal, a choice dictated partly by compulsion and partly on economic consideration, because the prohibited items involved an extra cost because of locational disadvantage.

Before any afternoon siesta, I thought I'll arrange for my evening sundowner, but my 'jugad' strategy was undergoing a severe test. The waiter at the lodge assured me that liquor could always be arranged with an hour's advance notice provided one was willing to bear the extra cost due to transportation and risk insurance. Extra cost would take the fun out of the evening drink, so I finally decided in favour of a voluntary compliance to the prevalent excise laws.

I had already ruled out the grass smoking option which I thought was infra dig for me. An indulgence fit for half – clad ash smeared wandering mendicants sitting next to their fire place.

The external stimuli for lifting the spirits already ruled out, I settled for the next best natural healthy option of an evening walk on the promenade along the Holy Ganges.

It was way back in 1903 that Dr. Weber a doctor in England in his empathy for old persons thought of means to make life healthier, happier and comfortable for them. Apart for repeating the dictum of 'early to bed and early to rise', moderation in eating and drinking, the principal recommendation was exercising the body through long walks. It was when you inhaled the best possible free access resource provided by nature. With access denied to motor vehicles on the promenade I could breathe to my heart's content in a relatively unpolluted environment without paying a penny.

It is unfortunate that humans often took a free access resource like clean and unpolluted air for granted, it's value realised only under some adverse circumstances. No wonder, Yoga system based the Prana, the vital life force in close conjunction with breath inhalation and exhalation.

I had partially sacrificed my afternoon siesta in favour of the evening walk and just taken a handful of water from the Ganges to wipe my face, symbolically washing away my sins by bird style Kak Snana.

On a cement bench on the banks of Ganges, above the stairs of the bathing ghat, I saw a foreigner clad in Yellowish Kurta and Pyjama, staring at the river in a contemplative mood. Instinctively I greeted him, exchanged smiles and after seeking his permission sat next to him.

The soulful evening which subsequently changed the course of my life was about to begin. Was this meeting with Leonardo fated or mere coincidence. Till date I have been looking for answers to this question. His name was Leonardo Veritiero, somewhat of a tongue twister, which meant a truthful person, strong like a lion. For some persons, the name conveys the personae of an individual. Physically he was tall and slim, but wore a very serene expression on his face.Leonardo was a marine engineer by profession who had been visiting Rishikesh for last four years during his annual holiday from work. Being a marine engineer he could not have escaped the post mortem report of Titanic. A ship which even God did not have the capacity to sink, perished in the ice cold waters of North Atlantic ocean leaving more than fifteen hundred people dead – considered to be one of the worst peacetime maritime disaster. Giant ship with so many fail safe mechanisms could not withstand an equally giant iceberg. The disaster was followed with many enquires to find out its cause. Whether the crew maneuvering the ship followed the standard operating procedures or were negligent, whether there were enough life boats for the safety of the passengers, how the material changed its properties and in ice cold water became brittle from ductile, water compartments sealed also got flooded due to design deficiencies.

It was said that at the look outs in the crow's nest there were no binoculars, therefore the iceberg was not visible from a distance and by the time it wanted to skirt the iceberg starboard side scraped along the iceberg causing rupture in the water tight compartments.

Inconscient metal had changed its behaviour, became brittle so as not to absorb the energy of impact and a collision led to the disaster.

The problem with the iceberg is that only one tenth of it is visible to the naked eye while nine tenth remains concealed under the surface of water. However, with advancement of technology, the hidden part can also be detected by radars on the sonar system. At times they produce a high pitched hissing sound called 'bergy seltzer' due to release of high pressure air bubbles from the ice as it melts into water.

However, the ice berg can be located whether above or below the surface of water because it is a material formations which is subject to sensory perception directly or through instruments or sensors.

What if it was accompanied by non –detectable, non – material force fields, benevolent or malevolent, what would have been the ship's fate?

A material substance like iceberg where the tip is visible has the potential to wreck a carefully designed luxury liner like Titanic, then what would be the potential constructive or destructive of non material invisible forces where even tip is not to be seen. The ship of life has to contend with iceberg both with its material and non-material form, mind lacking in capacity to detect it, then entire life becomes a very risky affair. But the mind has an unrealised potential, iceberg like, nine – tenth of it veiled and has to be upgraded from one tenth limited finite to an upgraded infinite, leading from bondage to freedom. It ceases to be mind and coalesces with Aatma – all knowing consciousness.

It is an obstacle course where the moments you clear one hurdle, next one is in sight calling for greater caution and perseverance.

Strangely, trying to seek answers to a technical or non-technical problem of a marine engineer perplexed by the forces of nature was the motivation which brought the foreigner to this far off place in India.

First fundamental lesson, yet the most important one which he learnt in the Ashram was about Shravan, Manan and Nidhiadhyasan, keep your ears and eyes open, let every perception seep in as deep as it can, cognise, think and try to understand, the process of contemplation and having understood the process of contemplation and start meditating. Life had offered him a chance. It was for him to accept and grab it. Here was the opportunity ringing at his door which he was more than willing to accept.

What do we call it, chance providence, coincidence, destiny or 'prarabdha' which determines the life cycle of an individual. The Karmik residue, good bad or in different.

Is there any substances in law of Karma, so or is it just a ruse to instill fear in the people to make them subordinate or motivate them to behave more sensible, ethically. There were questions galore to which he thought he may be able to get satisfactory answers. A technology optimist was also becoming a philosophical optimist, both subsisting side by side in their own domains.

As I entered the big auditorium like hall in its basic simplicity and sat on the matted floor facing the makeshift stage which was a low and wider wooden table on which rested a mattress covered by a sheet. There was a mike placed on it along with a glass of water. The master clad in a woolen saffron robe entered the hall. I felt, kind of mesmerised by the serene expression on his face, and imagined a halo around his face. There was pin drop silence in the hall and nobody in the audience was willing to make any movement lest it may cause any disturbance. The discourse had begun.

Au....mm (Om) the chant reverberated in the environment and the discourse began with the invocatory prayer of Brihadaranyaka Upanishad. 'The Upanishad of the great forest'. 'Om Purnamadah, purnamidam, purnat purnamudacyate, purnasya, purnamadaya, purnamevavasisyate. Om Shantih Shantih Shantih

That is the plenum of full. You take the full out from it, yet it continues to remain full. Om peace! Peace! Peace.

Infinite has no dimensions. It is dimension less beyond our comprehension. Therefore, there is neither any addition or subtraction from it because infinite is all inclusive. The story of the universe is the story of the incomprehensible infinite.

We look at the awe inspiring creation present before us as nature with its various hues and forms with wonderment, sensing it, cognising it. The perception leads to stimulation of all thought and emotion in us and a quest for its origin, the causal principle.

The scientists over the ages, experimented on the wonder of creation and then came to an inference that there existed an infinitely small but infinitely dense particle which about 13.4 billion years ago decided to explode.

Along with the energy and heat of explosion came the gases, suddenly from the infinite small particle was created space and time. As the temperatures came down, there was condensation of gases leading to liquid and solid matter.

So in scientific terms the Universe was born with the singularity of 'Big bang', the first fundamental principle of universe, the first scientific paradigm. Somehow it is surmised that life there after emerged from 'diluted rock soup' first as a unicellular organism, and thereafter Darwin and his followers took the baton and carried it forward.

In my humble opinion the singularity of Big bang is the paradox of infinite. Infinitely small is the minimum inconceivable while infinitely dense is the maximum inconceivable. The invocation which I recited in the beginning is a symbolic representation of the paradox by the philosophers. A science – physics which only accepted hypotheses, laws or theories which could be empirically verified went along merrily with the idea not only of infinitely small particle containing in itself the infinite seed or potential of creating a universe which according to the prevalent scientific thought is expanding. Nobody termed it as a superstition or miracle of miracles, a magical wonder. The paradox was as such accepted by the scientific community.

However, we as humans are curious people. In animals it is an instinct which is necessary for survival but we are endowed with a mind and intelligence which prevails over the instinct and often diluting it by reason.

There were a few in the scientific community who were curious about the condition antecedent. But Big Bounce, Big crunch or Big Bounce Big Crunch cycle could not capture the imagination of the researchers once Hubble came forth with the idea of 'the expanding Universe'. A few astronomical observations followed and the age of universe finalized. At last universe was born 13.4 billion years ago -period.

If matter could be designated as God, religion not withstanding this was the ultimate doctrine of scientific theism.

Once the universe was born then onwards starting from Aristotelian dynamics and Ptolemy's astronomy to Hubble Heisenberg Feynmann Schroedinger via Kepler Galileo Newton Einstein Planck and numerous others whose curiousity prompted them to delve into the unknown occult. Thus, proceeding in a systematic scientific manner we have come a long way trying to explain the phenomenal world as we perceive it. However, we are yet to locate the elusive Higgs Boson, which the scientific community feels will settle the riddle of the universe, unless it raises new question which the scientists of the future will be busy seeking the answers.

Why should we waste energy and time to explain the 'antenatal condition' because even the discovery of 'a complete unified theory' may not aid the survival of our species or may not even affect our life style, so why bother about. Haeckel was right when he said that why try to find out about the 'thing in itself' the 'noumenal' of Kant when we don't even know whether it exists or not.

However the Rishi – the poet seers of ancient India thought somewhat differently 'Naiveha kinchanam agre asit? What existed prior to creation? Nothing absolutely nothing except for a devouring all consuming death principle 'ashnaya mrityuh'. A condition of total non – objectivity. It was all enveloped in darkness because God had not yet said 'Let there be light'.

Neither a subject nor an object, neither a seer nor anything to be seen. It was the light of darkness incapable of being perceived by the senses.

While the physicists was looking for the elusive matter particle, Rishi the Indian meta physicist was perplexed about the 'original ubiquitous continuum' an integral existence consciousness infinite, ineffable, indescribable, which by the will and force of its own being gets differentiated into multiple forms, one becoming the many. Rishi was getting more curious, uneasy, uncomfortable. Out of this sense of dissatisfaction and inquisitiveness started emerging the Indian philosophy. Bewildered by the universe along with physics, philosophy along with metaphysics was born.

An innocent ignorant yet curious youngster asked the intelligent, knowledgeable and experienced ones, supposedly knowers of the Brahman, the Absolute, the fundamental question. What is the ultimate causal principle of which the phenomenal universe is the effect. Where have we come form and where to would we ultimately be going. Who is the supreme producer director of this entire life drama which we know very little about.

The wise ones the masters were momentarily non – plussed. Where did the answers lie to these vexed questions of here in before, life and here in after birth, life and death. Here emerged the principle of negation 'Neti, Neti' not this not this. All that they told the young aspirant that factors like time, nature, destiny, accidental chance, physical objects and objectiveness were ruled out. No positive answers were forthcoming, yet needing an explanation of sorts.

Newton thought of light travelling in ether as corpuscles, then the scientific community discarded ether which bounced back in its new incarnation as space time continuum, a more complex and more evolved form, creating an altogether new paradigm.

The scientists were quite perplexed which made Schroedinger say that consciousness cannot be accounted for in physical terms. Jung the psychologist of the new era also felt that curiousity is gradually shifting from material externals to subjective internal.

With the advent of theories of relativity, uncertainty and indeterminacy, assertion of consciousness as a fundamental principle, the dividing lines between physics and metaphysics were getting blurred.

Coming back to curious young lad unable to get satisfactory positive answers, at least knew as to where not to look for, the excluded domain.

What is going to be his next move, we will discuss it tomorrow.

The over powering aura in the prayer hall kept me mesmerised during the discourse, and I woke up as if from a trance when Leonardo tugged at any arm and I realised we were among the last ones to leave the place.

The desire for alcohol had evaporated and for me, the philosophy had been born, now it needed to be understood in the years to come.

I accompanied Leonardo to a nearby eating joint which served a vegetable minestrone soup along with some pasta in a basil pesto which had a hint of mint.

Coming back to the lodge, I retired to bed early, something alien to my normal habit. Perhaps the after effect of the discourse.

Master's words that the world of soul nestled in the seemingly dark cave of heart is much more fascinating than all the so called pleasurable objects of the phenomenal world which we encounter in our work a day life were reverberating in my mind.

In my curiosity propelled enthusiasm, I along with Leonardo despite his protestation was among the earliest entrants to the prayer hall. The discourse like yesterday began with the chant of 'Aum' and the invocation prayer about the infinite.

Coming back to the problems of the novitiate aspirant, where the answers were all in negations also explains the dilemma of the teacher. How to describe indescribable infinite noumenal, the thing in itself in finite phenomenal terms.

The Lord which determines, causal principle is addressed to as Brahman, but there the sight travels not, speech, mind,ear and senses have no access. It is neither known and is beyond the unknown, how do you know the Knowledge perse. It's not an object, yet there is a mind that one should utilize. The highest possible faculty of knowledge we have is our mind. But when the knowledgeable ones hold the view that our limited mind fails because 'that' is the mind of the mind. How does the effect enter the cause. An absolute catch 22 situation.

Philosophically it is the epistemological predicament. How do you know anything? It is the problem of knowledge, Kant the Copernican Philosopher provided the cue by his idea of transcendental unity of apperception. Yet stopped short of entering the domain of the noumenal but Rishi's of yours, poet seers in their intuitive vision had inferred that mind can be up graded and be infinite. It has the capacity to transcend the space time and can enter the planes of higher consciousness where names forms, appearances tend to disappear. It is the domain of the real. Satyam Gyanam Anantam Brahman, Truth, knowledge infinite or Satchidanand, Existence consciousness bliss.

Having thought of the destination, the path needs to determined and objective finalized, the methodology has to be worked out.

How the limited sensory and mental spectrum has to be widened so that all the ultra violets and infra reds are within the domain. This simple yet complex praxis or methodology was termed as yoga by Rishis – who were among the first Indian psychologists, ones who had anticipated Freud, Adler, Jung and proponent of Psi centuries back. It culminated in meditation.

In deep meditation the aspirant, the seeker became aware of 'Devatma Shakti' the power of the Lord hidden in itself. The primal causal principle. The cosmic mind, cosmic idea and all its manifestations constituting the phenomenal world become clear. It is the super mind guided by the Aatma the self.

Why is it that the novitiate had to meditate to understand the structure and operation of the universe, to unravel it mysteries and to solve it's riddle? Is it in the realm of practicality. Can there be vision of divinity? Very perplexed issue, but the simple answer is yes, but with lot many provisos.

What is Yoga and why it is necessary to follow the path to understand the universe. It is simple harmonizing my individuality a partite ego dominated existence with the cosmic ego, individual consciousness with the cosmic or universal consciousness, like the river losing its identity entering the ocean or in a positive way expanding its identity from one of the rivers to the entire ocean.

The limitation of mind is the veil of ignorance which conceals the ultra violets and infrareds. Avarana – veil and Vikshepa – fickleness of mind leading to lack of concentration and dissipation of energy. Yoga as harmony through techniques of concentration is based on the law of conservation of energy.

Dharma – the universal law of righteousness has been summarised as the law of sacrifice, Yagya – yag, whereby individual limited consciousness becomes universal consciousness by sacrificing the ego the 'I ness', the differentiating factor between I and You.

It is a new way of understanding where by the great sentence of the Vedas 'That thou art', starts making sense.

How can I be equated with you by a law of identity between two entirely different things.

Yes says Yoga. What was non – sensical in the phenomenal world makes total sense in the spiritual domain. The great scriptures called 'Shrimad Bhagwat Gita', the 'song Divine' has been interpreted in the terms of the great sentence which I mentioned. The first six Chapters relating to 'Thou' and next six to 'That' and final six establishing a harmonious relationships between the two in which they merge into each other. What a wonder, Yoga is, from a problematic relative phenomenal world to an Absolute blissful Noumenal cosmic consciousness. But there is a big caveat, of which I will talk about a little later.

Yoga, then is a game of harmony. Harmony with in and harmony without. The differentiation between what we consider internal to us and what is external gets obliterated. It is 'Samatva' – a balance an equipoise. Nothing is internal, nothing external, one grand all inclusive organic whole.

It raises a very interesting question. Why with a little effort every denizen of this world of mortality become an immortal yogi. What happens to the world when everyone becomes a yogi, back to the primitive days of living by nature. Gatherer only because hunting option gets closed and there are no farmers, no cattle rearing, no alms givers, no textiles. But anticipating the situation says the grand scripture Gita that such an eventuality is never going to arise.

Now the provisos have their field day. One it is a tremendous effort where in the end body, mind, life and intellect get entirely transformed while ego gets neutralised.

The fundamental principle of creation, differentiation of the integral by infusion of ego is negated. That's why it is tremendous effort coupled with deep detachment. All objects, all things material cease to exist, what remains is the inscrutable pure consciousness. Devatma Shakti the force field of Universal self. Energy perse or consciousness perse, which subsumes all things considered relevant or meaningful by us.

To be in a state of mind where we as the flowing waters of a river merge into a sea of consciousness as its wave, understanding the organic unity of the cosmos, this is meditation.

Thereafter followed as small story more in metaphors from Kathopnishad – the philosophical part of the Vedic text. Rather than history, mythology folklore it is the story of knowledge in its essence free from space time and personalities. It is the story of limitless profundities within man and universe rather than a perception of shifting scenes, events in space time and the under current normally known as history. It is a story of a person who realising the inadequacies of empirical experiences wants to go to the ultimate experience of truth, Absolute freedom from the cycle of birth and death.

It is the story of Nachiketa, a brilliant young Brahmin, son of Vajashravah –a typical man of the world, one who is desirous of earning merit by gifting Vaj, Anna – the material things to others following the performance of a Yagya – a sacrificial ritual. Law of sacrifice Yagya, along with law of Karma and overriding universal law of righteousness called the law of Dharma, have dominated the Indian philosophical scenario for ages.

Law of Sacrifice stipulates that you sacrifice your most prized possession, which is dear to you. However, what was being gifted by the Vajashravah were old cows which had stopped giving milk and were more of liability rather than utility to the person who accepted. Nachiketa realizing the falsity of the ritualistic offerings by his father, that his father was more likely to get demerit and ignominy rather than merit and fame. While pointing out the folly to his father he incurred the wrath of his father and cursed to death. So he landed up at the door of Yama, the Lord of Death in the yonder world. Lord of Death was away on some errand so the young lad had to spend three nights without any food or water at the doorstep of Yamas residence. When Yama came back and realised that the young Brahmin boy had been there for three days, unattended to by anyone, he was repentant and profusely apologised to the youngster. A Brahmin guest like Brahmin fire which if not properly attended to can cause extensive damage, consume all your physical possessions, so Yama immediately offered some water to quench his thirst and thereby douse the fire to save his possessions. As a compensation for withstanding the pangs of hunger for three nights, the youngster was granted three boons.

Nachiketa, in the first boon wanted to be sent back to his father in the world and wanted to be greeted and accepted back with love and affection. This lays the basic foundation of Yoga in this world. It is the boon for being in total harmony with the world – samatva. No conflicts, no anger, no delusions.

The second one was about the knowledge of 'Fire – sacrifice' which led humans to pleasures of heaven coupled with a state of relative immortality like those of the celestials, which lasted for a Kalpa a cycle of creation. Granted said the Lord. The youngster by now had the knowledge of relative immortality and having entered the abode of Yama had also experienced the reality of death.

The third boon was yet to come. Not fully satisfied with the idea of relative immortality, he wanted the knowledge of absolute immortality beyond the cycle of birth and death 'the great beyond'.

Yama tried his best to dissuade him by offering various tempting alternatives, kingdom of the earth with all its appurtenant wealth, a long life with a strong and healthy body, celestial maidens with their chariots and musical instruments in attendance, practically all the pleasures and joys of a worldly life one could ever think of. Nachiketa saying that no man can remain happy for ever by wealth and possession which are ephemeral in nature, rejected the offer out right. His argument was very simple. Nobody anywhere could be more competent a teacher than Lord of Death to explain the concept of death and immortality and he refusing to grant the boon, to whom does he go to find the answers to the vexed question of 'final death' and 'absolute immortality'. Yama, satisfied about the sincerity and credentials of the youngster agrees to the knowledge about the mystery of death and 'great beyond' which superceded, birth, death and rebirth.

There is an argument called the 'ontological argument' which in simple terms means whether god exists or not. It has been debated by philosophers mustering equally convincing arguments for his existence and counter arguments for non –existence yet it continues and likely to continue for ever without any firm conclusions. This was question even deeper than the ontological argument as to whether soul exists or not.

Yama begins his discourse to answer the question. There are two paths, preyas the path of worldly pleasure the pleasant one but temporary transient, the other is shreyas – intrinsically good, everlasting. The choice is yours. You may accept the visible as the real and nothing exists beyond that. But the truth is that invisible is the real – in the sense that it is eternal everywhere, not confined to a single location at a single moment.

Here is introduced Yoga more as a mental process, a psychological effort in exercising your choice. As a pathway to truth, reality or perfection. Arise awake and find a teacher, the most competent, guide, mentor, an aid because it is the most arduous path, like a razor's edge. You shed all the baggage of your ego and approach with maximum humility. It is an ascent where the body, the gross physical, mind the subtle physical, the psychology and finally the spirit have to be disciplined. The 'Mysterium Tremendum' gets unraveled by greatest of efforts. Three days of fasting by Nachiketa in the absence of Yama symbolize austerities, first disciplining the body, then the mind and finally the spirit. This is where the law of sacrifice operates in all its glory. Yagyo vai Vishnu – Sacrifice is Lord himself the sustainer. It is the supreme effort of soul in its march to reach the ultimate destination, the great beyond.

However, ordinary rational logic fails so does the intellect, the highest faculty, yet it is possible to go beyond the intellect.

Our mind has the capacity to resonate with the cosmic mind much more superior than the human mind provided the frequencies match. The methodology to transform individual mind to understand things in the universal or cosmic mind does it is the arduous path of yoga which is suggested. The mind considering its self as sovereign in this world becomes subordinate to Aatma or self and there by river being part of the ocean adds tremendously to its limited dimension. This is what is meant by a mantra Abhyarohan Pavman which says let me be led from darkness to light, from non – existence to existence, from death to immortality.

What adds to one's difficulty is that it is not a straight forward linear visible path with milestones depicting the distance to the destination. No signages, no maps except for sharing of experiences with those who have tried to tread the path earlier. The Guru, the dispeller of darkness, men of wisdom are able to provide guidance. There is absolutely no physical movement. Progress if at all can be thought of in psychological terms. –Intellect, logic fail here, what is needed is Gods grace. Destination is neither a place nor an object nor a person. It is the indefinable absolute. The first and foremost requirement is peace and harmony, absolutely no Vikshepa or disturbance in body, senses, mind or intellect. A clear vision by way of practice of psycho – physical purity, a composed personality seeking support from all quarters, whether earth, heavens or sky. All the presiding principles of senses and mind and intellect, the gods need to bless us and therefore have to propitiated by purity of thought. This is where Sadhana, the deployment of means assumes great importance. In order to be eligible for integral experiences – intuitive revelation, Yoga becomes the purificatory process, a method of conscious expansion of consciousness. It is said by the masters that 'thou' part – the first six Chapters of Gita are all about self – integration by way of spiritual discipline.

Enemy armed with objects promoting lust, anger, attachment, fear, all kinds of emotions which can befuddle your reason, intellect, and equipoise are ever willing to shoot their arrows. It is the battleground Kurukshetra, land of sacrificial ritual of the gods, where you are thrown off your feet at any moment. How do you stay put struggling for spiritual survivals in the slippery ground of phenomenal World. This is the battle of Mahabharata.

Is there a soul or not? Yes say the scriptures, religious scriptures and philosophical texts. All evidence is either direct or by inference or by accepting an authoritative source becomes important. Then why can't we see it or be aware of it? Because it belongs to the domain of unknown, unknowable in the ordinary sense. Nine – tenth of the iceberg is below the surface of water and only one – tenth visible to eye. So is the case with the universal. Only the immanent manifested part is visible and limitless infinite is inconceivable.

Where does the key lie to solve the riddle of life which also is the riddle of the universe.

We will continue tomorrow. It took me a little time to emerge out of some kind of hypnotic influence which the words had. Before I proceed to the next story which was part of the discourse next day, I thought picking Leonardos mind, a person who had been attending these sessions and had old association's with the speaker about the issues which had been discussed during last two days, starting with the concept of starting the session with a chant.

A person with a different ethnicity, cultural background, and value systems, yet enamoured of spirituality, a keen observer of things would be ideal person to answer some basic question and would ultimately help me in getting to the master for a one to one dialogue.

Leonardo said that we have to go to the initial vibration. The first product of space emerging from the subtle principle of vibration – sound. This was the Planck's epoch – time begins now.A period dominated by the quantum effect of gravity according to physics and space time according to Indian philosophy. Once the space time was there, a movement began sparsha, the subtle tactile principle led to air and air movement led to – Rupa the subtle form of fire principle out of which emerged the heat due to friction Agni, and subsequent condensation the subtle principle of rasa, liquid led to water. By now sub atomic and atomic particles had come to existence and the subtle principle of smell led to matter which symbolized by the earth. It included the stars, galaxies everything which was material.

It started with a timeless, space less, ubiquitous energy or a unmanifested force field termed as consciousness, leading to the manifested form which we terms as universe. The primal vibration symbolic of the creator was termed as Aum. The first letter A corresponding to the waking state, U for the dream state and M for the state of deep sleep. The Amatra Viram-quantum less silence thereafter representing Turiya, the transcendent state.

So it all began from a word, 'Let there be light' and there was light. Sound Tanmatra the subtle principle of space marks the beginning.

The primal Vibration of the Universe, includes all the effects which include space, time, atmosphere or gases Fire, water and solid matter.

Aurobindo in his commentaries and interpretations of the Vedic treatises and Upanishads followed a technique whereby he divested the meaning of words according to its modern notions and went into the context of early Vedantic use of words, and in interpreting the verses of Kena Upanishad treated word as the creatrix as in the Vedic system. From ideation at a transcendental level to an energy vibration in the gross sound form, expressed as speech from Para to Vaikhari.

Letter is called Akshara, that which is imperishable. Cosmic Word emanating from the cosmic idea or cosmic mind is the intrinsic reality of every object. All objects are the representative forms of the cosmic idea in terms of words. It's the energy the vibration which creates or destroys. Speech creates forms of emotion, mental images and an impulsion to act. This creative act of speech forms the basis of theory of Mantra. Underlying it is the principle that word of power emanates from a level of consciousness which is deeper of the Being. It emanates from a layer which is deeper than the intellect, closest to the self. It is more potent in its silence, thatswhy a mental chanting is considered to be superior. The Mantra has the power to create new subjective states in ourselves. It has the potential to alter our psychical being by broadening our mental spectrum. It has the capacity to vitalize and change the atmosphere.

Once a disciple asked his Guru as to what Absolute was all about. The Guru with his eyes closed was perhaps contemplating, so no answer came. After a while the disciple repeated the question in a slightly louder tone. Again there was no answer. Then disciple waiting for a while against asked the question in a much louder tone. The Guru opened his eyes and said, I have been answering the question all this while, yet you refused to understand. It is silence, Absolute silence, because it cannot be described in words.

Shruti – the Vedas as knowledge is called the rhythm of the infinite heard by the soul.

So these discourses led to my attitudinal change.

As a teacher in a college teaching history I decided at the age of fifty to quit and came to this place. Since I never got married, so I had no family liabilities.

Chapter - 13

WHERE DO WE BEGIN

Rohit began his discourse.

Where do we begin? Let us start with 'mysterium tremendum et fascinans' - a mystery which attracts, which repels and is at root of all philosophy, scientific, pseudo scientific or unscientific termed according to interpreter's own proclivities.

'Who am I'? a question which can be answered in multiple ways. I have eyes which can see the world around, but they cannot see themselves. So how do I describe my identity. I can't look into myself, senses fail. So I have to take recourse to some other method. The method is called self analysis. Let us start with simple answers. I am an individual part of a species called Homo sapiens, which means I am a hominid and I am sapient endowed with intelligence. The evolutionary scientists say that our species is only surviving hominid with a simian ancestry. Our simian ancestry traces it's origin to tree shrews and lemurs. Our great grand ancestor was an unicellular living organism with survival instincts strong enough to get finally transformed into Homo sapiens. How did life enter into? It's been explained by some chemical reaction in 'diluted rock soup' under particular conditions. The mystery would get clear in times to come, say the scientific optimists. In course of evolution following the principles of struggle of existence and survival of the fittest with some modifications, additions and deletions from time to time, some different individualities in term of species or genera were created, some disappeared, some survived. It was a gradual ascent from elemental mineral to plants to animals, sub humans to human. A process which perhaps followed certain laws of nature, some known and understood, some unknown as yet involving millions of mutations, transformations, birth, death through ages. It is said that there have been mass extinction events where a large part of the bio-diversity disappeared altogether. The giant dinosaurs, physically very strong just could not survive.

According to scientists it began billions of years ago and humans are an intermediate stage. Where do we go from here?

Homo Deus, Homo Perfectus and finally Perfecto Perfectus- the infinite all inclusive Absolute.

Rishi's of yore contemplated on it and came to a conclusion that evolution is a process of ascent of consciousness, starting from near inconscient matter to divided consciousness of humans and teleological march ends at an indescribable pure consciousness.

What we encounter in this world as a phenomenon is the gross manifestation of the subtle and conversely subtle is the essence of gross. So all evolution is an ascent from gross to subtle and the involution part of the cycle was descent of subtle consciousness into grosser form of matter. This is what has been described in scriptures, especially the Vedic literature as a creation cycle, cosmological descent to the level of inconscient or almost veiled rudimentary consciousness and thereafter the ascent being according to certain laws of nature.

It raises a fundamental question as to who is the formulator of these laws and who is the supreme regulator. Secondly if there be a Supreme intelligence creator, God so as to say, then what is the need for creation, this recurrent cycle of involution and evolution. Since the world or universe exist, whether as reality or appearance., it needs to have an explanation for it. A need has always been felt to posit a conscious force, intelligence and absolute power to explain it, and there enters religion bringing with it a God into our lives. The very term God has theistic connotations, something not very palatable to a class of scientists. Atheism or agnosticism give rise to the theories where there is a denial of God, because the very concept of God in their opinion does not emerge out of accepted rational logic and is not subject to empirical verification.

This material monism or a strange kind of scientific theism, if I may call it, has done great service to the humanity because of it's limitations and quest for a thing which cannot be explained in the scientific theories continues, whether it be in the material domain or the psychic domain.

The Indian philosophical thought in its glory combined with mythology, therefore posited a triad of creator, sustainer and destroyer. Brahma, Vishnu, Rudra Mahesh. One question still remains unanswered in spite of positing the trinity of God. What was the need to create, sustain and dissolve and continue the cycle. Here 'Big-Bang' and 'Big crunch' cycle does not need an explanation in terms of a creator or destroyer because it follows the natural laws, but it does not eliminate the need for a law giver and regulator. If we assign that supreme power to nature then it can be expressed as 'God' Omnipresent, Omnipotent and Omniscient.

The Indian philosophers were no less scientific in their approach. While the modern scientist started from the gross and moved to the subtle from molecules to atom to protons, electrons and quarks and various theories like string theory and beyond and leaving a gap where things were uncertain or indeterminate, the sage philosopher started from 'Sukhshmati suksham Kalilasya Madhye' subtlest of the subtle in a non material potential from getting manifested in grosser forms. His imagery,symbols metaphors were different. His equations did not use the Greek symbols of alpha and omega. It was universal portrayed as a sacrificial horse. That transition from pure consciousness -all inclusive conscious force field, neither static nor dynamic, infinite inexplicable and indescribable in finite terms taking recourse to symbols, allegories and metaphors.

He started his probe into the fundamental cause. Is it Brahman? What kind of cause? Material or efficient or both, what life is all about? Where have we come from and where do we go from here? What is herein before and what is herein after? Do the subtle soul survive death of the grosser form named body? Is it a complete annihilation where nothing survives, from dust we are born and unto the dust we go- period. Who is the supreme producer director of this life drama apparently beginning with birth and ending with death.

Even the wise ones had no answer. All they could say was it is not time, inherent nature. or destiny, accidental chance or elements of matter or an elemental womb or a person which could be considered as a cause. It is neither a combination of all these. The individual self is also eliminated because it is not free, subject to pleasure and pain.

We are in a blind alley. Where do we go from here? Where do we find our answers?

On own real self acts as the laboratory. In deep meditation, the realization dawns on the self that it is Devatma Shakti, the creative divine power hidden in its own qualities which is the primal cause. There follows the analogy of a wheel Brahma Chakra wherein on a single rim are three circular tyres, sixteen extremities, fifty spokes, twenty fasteners, six sets of eight strengthening it, driven along three different paths with the support of a single yet manifold word and a delusive single revolution that gives rise to all dualities like pleasure and pain.

Now comes the description of the symbols. Rim-denotes the infinite potential of creation or nature, the three tyres represent the three qualities of nature Sattva, Rajas and Tama, as well as time, space and causation. The sixteen extremities represent five elements, five sense organ, five action organs and mind. The fifty spokes were symbolic of five viparyaya or ignorance or misapprehension and twenty eight ashaktis or disabilities and nine tushtis or contentment or satisfactions. Twenty counter spokes are the ten senses and their ten objects. The six sets of eight factors includes Prakriti Ashtaka-eight fold nature which include the five element, mind, intellect and egoism, Dhatu-Ashtaka-the eight constituents of body like skin blood flesh fat bone marrow semen etc, Ashta Siddhi- the eight supernatural powers, Bhava Ashtaka-eight mental states celestial deities and finally Guna Ashtaka, the eight virtues or noble qualities. The single cord desire is the one which binds all in this world. The wheel of Truth is driven over three paths. The path of Dharma righteousness, Adharama- unrighteousness and Jnana- path of knowledge.

This is the revolution of the wheel, cycle of birth and death, also the cause of vice and virtue. The entire life cycle with its strengths and frailties, is contained in just one verse. That is where the guru steps in to interpret it in the right manner.

The sage philosophers thought is not limited to physical nature, space or time. It transcends physicality and enters the transcendental domain. This is what distinguishes him from a modern scientist. He enters into the domain of metaphysics while trying to identify the causative factor or realm – the noumen which governs the phenomenal world. It is self analysis when we dive deep into ourself and as microcosm, a miniature replica of macrocosm try to find answers to the vexed questions of life and beyond.

The modern scientist is constrained by the concept of empiricism, where crossing its boundaries the scientists feels that he lays himself to charge of being unscientific, something unverifiable in the scientific laboratory, becomes speculative and illogical.

However with Einstein, Max Planck, Heisenberg, Schroedinger, Minkowski, David Bohm, and host of others like Eddington and Alfred White Northhead the attitudes are changing. The theory of relativity special as well as general, changed the whole concept of space time. So much so, that Einstein's teacher Minkowski said that 'henceforth space by itself and time by itself are doomed to fade away into mere shadows, and only a kind of union of two will preserve an independent reality.'

Hubble said the universe is expanding and thereby changing every moment. Max Planck, who was very keen to study Physics, was advised by a professor that there is only one universe and alas it has already been discovered by Newton. So there is nothing left to be discovered. Yet Planck persisted with Physics and bought about The quantum Revolution followed by the concept of uncertainty and probability –a tentativeness regarding laws of Physics.

What do many astro-physicists of the modern era say? That about four percent of whole universe is ordinary matter; rest is 'dark matter' or 'dark energy'. No wonder Schroedinger inspired by the wave function collapse came around to the view that 'consciousness' is absolutely fundamental. 'It cannot be accounted for in terms of anything else'. The same sentiment was echoed by Roger Penrose when he opined about the 'non-computability' of consciousness.

Very few people realize that astrology which derived all its calculations from astronomy, was an important 'Vedanga' an auxiliary discipline of Vedas, and was forerunner of modern day astro-physics.

A gradual shift in scientific thought in the universe toward a bio-centric universe in indicative that it is as important to probe within as with out. The whole concept of yoga is about effacing the distinction between 'internal and external' and transformation from an individual to universal.

It is primarily the search for identity along with our relationship with the world, nature and God, which are viewed as external to us has given rise to various schools of Indian philosophy, orthodox as well as heterodox. The Indian philosophical thought tries to explain the evolutionary movement of the world towards an unknown destination. The whole creation including us is being experienced every moment of our life and we try to seek an explanation for it The Indian philosophical view point barring Lokayats or Charvaka, is that it is a psychological rather than material world, and draws a distinction between Ishwar shristi and Jiva shristi, God's creation and the one emanating from an individual mind.

In all our observations and experiences, we retain a small part, forget most of it with a new experience and seldom do the introspection and go into it's implications.

Masters say that we have a dual personality, holders of a dual citizenship. One of this phenomenal world as an ego-centric particular individual with a body mind and life, and other of the higher realm of pure universal consciousness as an immortal being with a soul which is divine.

This necessitates our self analysis and world analysis be done as a highly impersonal psycho analyst, without any subjective bias.

Our worldly existence is that of a limited being with a very limited mental and perceptional spectrum. We can only travel the distance which our mind and intellect can take us.

Chapter - 14

VEDANTA

What made you undertake a journey to this remote Himalayan village, when almost all old Indian scriptures regarding philosophy and psychology are available on the internet?asked Rohit. I was asked the same question in the resort near Corbett park. My answer there was different. My Rishikesh experience and a few interactions have given me some insight into the Indian way of philosophical thought. All the earlier debates among the scholars was more about their psychological and spiritual experience, empirical as well as trans empirical or worldly as well as beyond, rather than their textual knowledge. Experience sharing on a one to one basis perhaps is not practical or effective by a remote technological link. It needs to be person to person. Another important aspect was to test the validity of transference of spiritual knowledge by Shaktipaat, and such other tantric Yogic techniques. Are these the imaginary flights of fancy, or have some truth in it? Are there unknown spiritual dimensions which can be explored provided we can upgrade the capacity of our mind by Yoga. That's how Anna explained her visit to Tripatha.

Let me start with an outline of Vedanta- the philosophical teachings about spirituality which includes psychology.

Self analysis is the first step to self discovery and self realisation. Vedanta provides a solid philosophical framework for attainment of perfection by the knowledge path. Prasthan Trayi delineate the three fold knowledge path.

The foundational texts are Upanishads- upadesha prasthan or shruti prasthan. These are the Classical Vedanta texts which form the philosophical part of Veda, revealed and instructive. Since different Upanishads have been authored by different Rishis or sage seers, Brahma Sutra which reconciling the apparent contradictions presents it in a logical manner by way of aphorisms is the Nyaya Prasthan, and finally the Bhagwat Gita, synthesis of various knowledge philosophies is the Smriti Prasthan, secondary revelation based on memory.

While Vedanta provides the theoretical background, Yoga becomes the practical solution. Attainment of perfection by conscious integration of Being is the dominant theme of all major Upanishads.

We revert back to the earlier discussion regarding our quest for identity. Who am I? The Upanishads answer it by way of four great sentences-Mahavakyas.

Pragyanam Brahman, consciousness is the Absolute. Aham Brahmasmi, I am the Absolute. Tat twam Asi- Thou art That. Ayam Aatma Brahman- my Self is the Absolute.

This constitutes the great proclamation of Law of identity as different from Law of contradiction prevalent in this world. It brings forth the idea of knowledge by identity not by intellectual learning but by way of intuitive wisdom. It establishes my identity with God.

I, the immortal soul am one with him. The proclamation is based on an extensive logical analysis, by way of symbols, allegories and metaphors. It forms the core of Hindu philosophy, in its universality. It is valid for all times and all places, provided it is explained properly.

Vedic literature consists of four parts. The first two parts Samhita and Brahman texts are more about rituals and liturgy known as Karmakanda. Karma is Yagya Yaga, the sacrificial ritual and external and internal worship. The second part consists of texts known as Aranyaka and Upanishads. We gradually move from liturgy to philosophy- the Gyana Kanda. Empirical to trans empirical. From world and heaven to the unknown realms of consciousness. Vedanta starts with ritualistic symbols and then gradually takes to a higher level abandoning the rituals in favour of spirituality. Upanishads try to weave different threads of diverse colours into the unity of a supreme consciousness principle Brahman. It is Brahmavidya- the knowledge of the ultimate principle from which everything including the world nature and life emanates and gets dissolved in it at the end of a cycle. This is the infinitely small but infinitely dense singularity of big bang where everything exists in an un-manifested potential form.

Among the Samhita or treatises Rigveda lays the foundation for philosophy and the super structure with elaborate design and architecture is found in Upanishads.

Nasadiya Sukta talks of creation. What was there prior to creation? Nobody really knows. Even gods entered the scene later. Was it existence or non existence- a total void or nihil. It sowed the seed for metaphysics and philosophical brain storming.

The Hymn of Creation of universe goes into the condition precedent to the Big Bang. There was no space, no sky, neither death nor immortality, neither day nor night there was just One who breathed without air. It was darkness hidden by darkness and without distinctive marks it was all water, not the water we know of, it was ur water, a symbol of a strange kind of indescribable existence. From those waters the heat of tapas or penance brought forth this universe. Whether it was God's will or He was mute nobody knows. The Supreme Brahman of the world, all pervasive and all knowing, He indeed knows, otherwise nobody knows.

The philosophers of the future were left with a great riddle of the universe, to which they exercised their mind.

The baton had been handed over by the authors of Samhitas to authors of Upanishads.

Carl Sagan the modern astronomer found in the Hymn an example of Hindu tradition's skeptical questioning and unselfconscious humility before the great cosmic mysteries. The tradition was one of intellectual debate and questioning rather than imposition of absolute knowledge.

Vedantic doctrine starts with the premise that individual in this world is a limited being, whose mental and sensory spectrum is rather finite and limited. However his potential is infinite and the spectrum can be widened to illimitable dimensions. The basic method is of sense perception, contemplation and meditation. It is by way of intuitive wisdom that transcendent becomes understandable.

Let's start with the Upanishad and then move on to the other two texts of the triad.

All Upanishads reiterate the idea of unity of truth and multiplicity is just an appearance, transitory in character. The individual who perceives and the world which is perceived are mere projections of a universal consciousness, Brahman the only all inclusive reality or truth. It is integral, undifferentiated, non relational, non material, supra mental where knower, knowledge and known merge into a unity. Ekam Eva advitiyam, one without a second, non dual exhausts the possibility of a second. All names and forms appearing in the universe are relative and transitory and denoting a false appearance of truth. Self realisation leads to realisation of the Absolute, whose executive power or force is termed as God. Knowledge by means of meditation is the main path to attain perfection.

Upanishadic thought posits two fundamental concepts of Brahman and Aatma which mean the same. All great sentences and the texts convey the same. Etad vaitad- this verily is that. A perfect law of identity conveying a sense of quintessential unity of consciousness-the transcendental truth beyond all empirical experiences attainable by shedding of individual ego sense.

Starting with cosmology as an involution process whereby pure consciousness subtle to the extreme get denser in a material form, and then the evolution process starts at three levels- physical, mental and spiritual. The ultimate objective and destination is perfection-realisation of the Absolute. Meditation on the indescribable, indeterminate infinite attributeless Absolute is impossible, so either we start with Bhakti or worship by assigning attributes to the Absolute and meditate by using symbols. Various Upanishads talk about Vidyas which are about various meditational techniques.

Meditation is a spiritual process calling for great tenacity and highest effort. Contemplation on Existence Consciousness Bliss, all pervasive as Sarvam Khalvidam Brahmam is the highest form of meditation. Since Absolute is neither a subject nor an object, the meditation begins by concentrating on an object and then gradually ascending to higher forms and finally reaching a state of thoughtlessness. At this stage mind gets transformed into sublime, and form disappears. It is setting one's own self in tune with God, which becomes universally inclusive. Ritualistic worship with a sense of spiritedness is again a milder form of meditation, practical and improves a person's outlook towards life. It is like expressing and experiencing an unbroken love for an object. Even in your breathing you try to connect yourself with the Cosmic Prana or life force.

Coming to Shaktipaat, which involves the transfer of spiritual knowledge and power by the Guru to the disciple goes beyond the domain of intellect and reason, but Vedanta also transcends it by introducing the unknown dimensions in a state of supra consciousness. According to Gita you have the inherent capacity to upgrade your own self, by divinity within, to be your Guru by the path of action, combined with path of devotion.

A lot has been talked about power of thought and thought transfer in spiritual life.

Post- war psychology there has been a concept of tertiary cognition which incorporates primary cognition at the sub conscious level as well as secondary cognition at conscious level where ideation combines with critical reason.

This entire field of knowledge in various states of consciousness including Samadhi or Turiya denoting the transcendental state of supreme consciousness has been thoroughly analysed by the Indian sage seers. Their symbols have been different, Mantra replacing the mathematical equations, yet contentwise it operates in the infinite and timeless space.

One does no know whether it was destiny, coincidence or synchronicity as Jung would call it, when Sir John Eccles the neuroscientist met Friedrich Beck, the physicist more adept in Quantum Mechanics at a summer school in northern Italy, the outcome was a quantum mechanical explanation of neuro transmission and brain processes and new explorations in the field of consciousness. Every now and then there are new interpretations in regard to mental processes and its outcomes. Finite reality can be cognised and understood by the finite mind, but infinite reality can be understood by the infinite mind. Purify it and upgrade it is the solution provided by the Rishis.

Is a person totally helpless and powerless in front of a overpowering law of nature regarding cause and effect?

Inspired Rishi the Vedic sage was loud and clear when he said, " You the children of immortal bliss, hear from me about the Ancient One full of light, beyond all darkness, knowing whom you are liberated from cycle of birth and death. There is no other way out".

Children of immortal bliss, we all are divinities in this world, oblivious of truth of our existence due to ignorance.

Let me introduce Shrimad Bhagwat Gita, popularly known as Gita- the song divine.

According to Aurbindo it is a scripture which professes Vedantic yoga, an amalgam or rather synthesis of Karma yoga or yoga of action, Gyan Yoga or yoga of knowledge and Bhakti yoga the path of devotion. It covers such a wide range of philosophy and psychology that it often leads to interpretational conundrums. It has in it all elements of psycho analysis, analytic psychology, Gestalt psychology as well as transpersonal psychology. It includes the Indian orthodox philosophies like Sankhya and Yoga with a Vedantic doctrine trying to reconcile the denial of the Materialist with the refusal of the Ascetic.

Lord Krishna the Godhead is the teacher, mentor, spiritual guide, counsellor, psycho analyst and a charioteer on the battlefield. He reveals his glories and manifestations which leaves his human discipline Arjuna the warrior cum human disciple totally dumb founded.

With multiple definitions of Yoga, it finally explains that Yoga is the practice of Truth which can be visualised by knowledge by way of nishkama Karma- a sense of detached and desireless action coupled with e deep sense of devotion. It attempts to remove the inadequacies of prevalent philosophies by positing the highest soul or spirit Purshottam- perfect person. Highest Absolute which includes the all matter as well as consciousness. There is nothing outside it.

Chapter - 15

BHAGWAT GITA

Why is it that a copy of Bhagwat Gita kept in all rooms. Why not other scriptures?

It's really good that question came from you Anna?

Last night while taking a stroll in the campus you said that you were in a sense a die-hard Freudian at heart, because inspite of two of his favourite disciples Jung and Adler parting ways with him, he continues to be the founding father of psycho analysis. Although it is said that what determined Freud's choice of scientific career was an extremely flowery essay on 'Nature' attributed rightly or wrongly to Goethe. Science led to medicine and physiology to psychology. Psychology was then defined in purely neurological terms. Rest, as they is history. In the west, Psycho-analysis heralded the era of scientific examination of human mind.

I have a strange feeling that Freud must have had a dream as child which determined his destiny writ large as a psycho analyst. The dream may have got embedded in his sub-conscious somewhere and finally led to classic 'Interpretation of dreams.'

However, I will let you in to a small Indian Secret. Preceded by a few thousand years the author of Bhagwat Gita had assigned the role of greatest psycho-spiritual analyst to Lord Krishna- god incarnate.

Freud in one of his introductory lectures on psycho analysis told his students that he is going to start with a presumption that they know nothing and therefore they are all in need of some preliminary information.

He told them that they should not feel offended if he treats them as neurotic patients. The message was loud and clear. Neurotics were patients with some kind of abnormal psychology needing special care.

Thus psycho-analysis was supposed to provide psychiatry its missing 'psychological foundation.'

Freud had a problem at hand. Two basic premises of his theory were found socially offensive.

Bringing the 'unconscious' into the foreground and treating it more significant and important than the conscious evoked a reaction because of intellectual prejudice. Second, the idea of sexual impulse in its wider connotation as a causal factor for human behaviour and thereby for nervous and mental diseases offended the morality of the time. All talk of Sex, howsoever important needed to be brushed under the carpet, Freud held the view that the opposition to the recognition of strength of sexual instincts or importance of sexual life of individuals was more on the basis of aesthetic and moral ground, rather than based on sound logical arguments.

However when the scene shifts from Vienna to Kurukshetra everything becomes topsy turvy. A normal human is also treated as abnormal and the whole discipline of Yoga is a methodology to get over that abnormality which is intrinsic or inherent to the humans.

Malady changes so is the line of treatment. In Psycho-analysis there is an effort on part of the therapist to probe the unconscious and try to bring unconscious and sub-conscious to the conscious level. The patient may or may not cooperate. It's primarily the exchange of words and maybe some body language, experiences which may be insignificant from the patients view point but very relevant for his mental state.

The therapist has to very patient and discerning.

In psycho-spiritual analysis and consequent therapy in Gita, the therapist as Godhead is definitionally omniscient. The probe goes much deeper beyond the unconscious into the spiritual domain. It's a psycho-somatic cum metaphysical problem.

It was a totally disintegrated personality of a brave warrior, a general in the midst of two armies, seeing his kinsmen his cousins, elders, teacher eager to fight, he says that his limbs have become languid, mouth has dried up, body is trembling and there is horripilation. Somatic symptom of a much deeper malaise. Superstitious, he sees the omens to be adverse. Does not have the strength to holds his weapon. Weak to the extent that he is not able to hold his body upright. Coupled with the physical condition is the mental confusion. Mind unsteady, agitated chaotic, not in harmony with body or intellect.

Bewildered, deluded in a melancholy mood, loss of self-confidence, conduct bordering on cowardly unwarrior like behaviour while unconcerned about dereliction of duty- accepting defeat without fighting could not have been a worse insult for a warrior.

On a psycho-physical plane was it an anxiety neurosis or personality disorder? Which any human individual is prone to. A subjective distress arising out of the social context, fear of enemies, Bhisma, Dronacharya and Karna the warriors on the enemy side were the mightiest of the warriors of their time. He perhaps feared for his life. What is going to happen to his family if he dies in the battle.

Well, whether it is a story of a mighty warrior riding his chariot in the battle ground with divine Lord Krishna as a charioteer, or is it about the triumph and tribulations of a human spirit or soul struggling for salvation. Arjuna is the human representative with all his strengths and weakness, in the midst of a battle like struggle which the worldly life is, facing a violent crisis which the soul faces in its upward movement. Liberation or salvation freedom is not so easy to come by.

It needs tremendous effort perseverance, continuity with deep sense of detachment. Apparent incompatibility between mind and soul, where mind has to be upgraded and sublimed in order to bring harmony. A human, limited in capacity has to overcome it's resistance not by suppression but by sublimation. That is Yoga sublime.

For Arjuna it was 'the dark night of soul', Day-break was yet to there, when the upward path would be discernible. From darkness to light, from unreality of non-existence to reality of existence and death to immortality is the journey described in Abhyarohana Pavman, the elevating chant of Brihadaranyaka Upanishad. Arjun symbolized a mortal human living in a transitional world with limited capacities to face the challenges of life. It is my problem, your problem, everybody's problem, a human problem. A situation further complicated by troubles of conscience and confusion of mind. Our moods are relative to the condition through which our psyche passes in the process of evolution. The grand design purposeful called teleology is not easy to understand. In his bloated ego-sense, the individual never regards himself as a symbol of a universal purpose.

Arjun's predicament is that of a human who is as an ego-centric individual, and is also a unit of the social organization with various ties of kinship, with other units. And in this battle the opponents 'champions of unrighteousness' are his kinsmen, revered teacher, grandsires, cousins, and friends. As an impartial individual soldier championing the cause of righteousness, these entire social ties have to be 'cut asunder by the sword'. He feels that the fight for justice at a practical level is a fight for self interest, where the cost is very high and benefits in terms of right to rule minimal. The first immediate reaction is that how can one be happy killing his own kinsmen? Their hearts may have been vitiated by greed, yet by killing them, the family gets destroyed and so do the clan based basic principles of governance,which ultimately is likely to lead to total anarchy. Life for everyone becomes a living hell. By killing the respectable elders, the pleasures of wealth and desirable things will be drenched in blood? He feels it is better to live in this world begging like a renunciate than to kill. With a mind confused, beset with doubts, he finally surrenders himself to wise counsellor to suggest the way out for him. 'To be or not to be' – I am not able to decide. I surrender to you my teacher not as a friend but as a disciple.

Here Arjuna apparently in order to get rid of his grief rather than as aspirant to know the absolute, more out of circumstance than the epistemic curiosity had requested the friend to be a teacher. He had put in a formal request in true Vedic tradition except that in the battlefield he did not approach the Guru with sacrificial faggot in hand-again a Vedic practice.

The Guru had to be Brahmanishta as well as Srotriya, one who has had the God consciousness realization by way of intuitive wisdom and theoretical knowledge of scriptural texts.

Here the teacher was God incarnate himself who had not yet revealed his cosmic from and glories as God.

The Gods in the Indian Pantheon were, though treated as immortals in the heaven had a human façade and that's why the hero of Mahabharat had been sired by kings of Gods Indra. All Kunti's progenies- Yudishthira, Bhima and Arjuna had Lord of Death Yama as father of Yudishthira, Bhima Son of Vayu the wind god and Arjuna son of lord Indra the king.

Being the progeny of Kings of gods, Lord Krishna could visualize the potential courage of Arjuna. He exhorted him not to yield to unmanliness, bordering on impotency. The genes he had inherited were of heavenly god and an earthly mother. So the courage and bravery potential had to be extremely, high that's why he is often been addressed as Parantapa- the scorcher of foes.

All this while before laying down his divine bow in the midst of the armies Arjun was trying to justify his conduct for not taking up the arms against the felons on the pretexts of elders, teachers and kinsmen's whom he revered, to be on the enemy side but forgetting that they lent their strength and support to Adharama-unrighteousness. It was a battle between Dharma and Adharma. His moral justification for his conduct was based on love and compassion, import of which he himself was not fully convinced.

It was a case of profanity trying to provide a divine colour to baser emotions, trying to refer to bad omens. He wanted moral support from his friend guide and charioteer, but got severe admonition, downright insult for Anaryalike behaviour –unenlightened like which has going to bring him infamy. The impurities creeped into his psyche.

He takes refuse as a disciple of Lord because he is not able to find 'Dharma' –the universal law of righteousness which would validate his action –even killing in a battle howsoever venerable, anyone who is not on the side of Dharma. Dharma literally means that law which holds things together, the law, norm rule of nature action and life. The instrinsic, inherent nature of anything. Not so easy to explain. Religion also is called Dharma because it is the basic concept of Universal consciousness. It makes a person conscious of Universality of being.

Lord Krishna sure of the credentials of his disciple leads him on the path of Yoga –a process of integration, total harmonization within and without. He follows a Socratic methodology starting with addition subtraction to more complex quadratic equation, mixed matrix, vector dynamics. He has to make Arjuna understand Dharma 'the intrinsic law of Being'. The first initiation has to be on the concept of 'Thou' in its' widest possible connotation and into the concept of 'That', the divine absolute and Henceforth equate them as Tat twam Asi, 'Thou art That'.

'That' is the transcendental unity of consciousness, all inclusive infinite absolute which in its immanent form as particularized individuals, sentient insentient, from a grain of sand to the sapient humans appears as a multiplicity, caused by nescience, an ignorance eternal in nature.

Hamlet had a similar problem, but unfortunately he did not have access to a divine counsellor and went insane.

All texts on ethical behaviour and conduct lay down rules and norms for normal situations. There were rules for war in ancient times. An archer fought with an archer, a soldier fought with a soldier, a general with the general. One with mace fought a warrior with mace.

Gita presents an extraordinarily typical situation of a fratricidal war, where wise ones with belief in the law of righteousness perforce support the forces of Adharma. Does one follow the normal rules of ethical conduct or violate it in the greater interest of the society. It is a situation where the duty to lie and kill superceded the normal ethical conduct and the killer does not incur any sin.

In a philosophical context Gita is the story of a spiritual seeker, his struggle and resulting sorrow and delusion and subsequent enlightenment through the instruction of Lord Krishna, which initiates him to the law of Dharma righteousness, and doctrine of Karma or action and Yoga as philosophy and practice.

Anna had a question. It was the memory of the Munich massacre which still lingered in her sub –conscious inspite of all her efforts to wipe it away. Can violence whatever be the provocation, be justified in a so called civilized society?

Are we really civilized asked Rohit. What does civilization entail? According to Toynbee the historian when he talks of western culture it means western civilization. So culture and civilization became interchangeable. An essential difference according to him between 'the primitive societies' and civilized one is the direction taken by mimesis or imitation with a caveat 'as we know them'.

In a primitive society, mimesis is directed towards the older generations, dead ancestors unseen but not unfelt, thus trying to look towards the past, customs rules and tradition of the past and the societies remain static. In case of a civilized society mimesis is directed towards creative personalities who command a following because they are pioneers.'Cake of custom ' is broken and society is in a change and growth path. It neither encourages nor discourages violence. Perhaps violence is an essential element of the evolutionary mode of life. No nation at war ever claims to be an agressor. Even if it attacks it is to defend some values. It always claims to be on high moral ground. It gets eulogized as 'creative destruction.'

There has been and will continue for all time a debate between tradition and modernity. Tradition has been termed a 'communion with the past', by way of a continuing dialogue reinterpreting the past. This is where apart from the value judgement aspect creeps in values whether imparted individually or societally have a strong subjective bias, specially with regards to traditions good, bad, or indifferent, partly because tradition creates a sense of cultural identity.

Something the individual or society can hold on to, which it feels makes him stronger visa vis the others. Security of the numbers. Value systems can be classified as absolute or relative in accordance with Dharma. Truth Righteousness will always be of eternal value, because it is a universal law, not a man made one where definitions and terms are changeable. It is not within the human capacity to change the law of gravitation, or laws of motion or thermodynamics or electro-magnetism. The interpretations may change the basic law continues to be the same.

Let me tell you the interesting story, said Rohit, of Kaushik the learned Brahmin and Dharma Vyadh, the righteous butcher selling meat. Kaushik involved in penance was sitting under a tree contemplating on the Absolute. Droppings of a stork perched on a branch fell on his head. He just could not control his anger and cast his fiery gaze on the stork which got reduced to ashes. After a while he felt repentant, but nothing could be done to restore the life of the innocent stork. He one day begging for alms with his begging bowl approached a Grihini-housewife. She welcomed him. Wile he was standing there, her husband came back from work and she became busy offering her husband food and other duties as a housewife. She apologized to him for delay in attending to the Brahman who against cast the fiery gaze on her. But it did not work this time. Grihini said that I am not a stork whom you killed for no valid reason. I perform my duties Swadharma as a housewife to the best of my ability. My primary duty as a housewife is to look after husband and family, then the others. Kaushik was surprised as to how the lady came to know about the stork incident. He never thought in terms of duty as enshrined in the law of Dharma. That was what had imparted the strength to Grihini that she could easily withstand the fiery gaze of the Brahmins. Kaushik was now at the receiving end. She directed him to a butcher selling meat in Mithila town, capital of Videha to understand the concept of Dharma, its subtler aspects.

Brahmin realized that stork was not at fault. Tree was his natural habitat and dropping its waste was natural. It was Kaushika who had entered his territory and failed to understand subtle dharma. His egoistic rage prevented him from right understanding. Grihini, though never witnessed the burning of stork knew about it on the strength of her Tapas-right performance of her household duties. All knowledge is about life, and life in anchored in the household. You don't have to be a forest dweller to understand Veda -the knowledge.

Kaushik, a bit disturbed conscious of his own weakness finally decided to visit Dharmavyadha. He went near the shop and stood at a distance. Dharmavyadha had a number of customers who were buying meat. After he attended to all his customers he noticed the Brahmin standing at a distance. You must be the Brahmin which the Grihini has sent. Meat shop is not the proper place to discuss subtleties of Dharma.

He requested him to accompany him to his home. Kaushika again was surprised and puzzled. The meat seller already knew the purpose of his visit without him talking about it and the Grihini incident. He accompanied Vyadha to his house and was offered a seat. The atmosphere in the house was quite different. It exuded a sense of purity Sattva. Kaushika asked Vyadha that how come a knowledgeable person like you is involved in selling meat, not a very noble profession. 'This is my Kuldharma' replied Vyadha and following your duty enshrined by you karma of the past, there is nothing demeaning about it.

Kaushika raised the question of non-violence. 'How could Dharmavyadha, so sensitive to Dharma could be very insensitive when it came to violence. Vyadha made it clear that duty as enshrined in Swadharma was a result of cosmic scheme of things, and acts performed in the past. That is what determined a person's station in life. The karmik liabilities of the past have to be discharged in the present life but there is a certain degree of freedom of action. Action can never cease but it does not become a liability if it is done with a sense of duty and with a sense of detachment. Kaushika realised that determining violence or non-violence is not easy. It is in mind that the idea of non-injury be nurtured. Once the principle of sacrifice is accepted and things enjoyed in the spirit of detachment and absence of greed and principles of life laid down by the cosmic power, one does not incur any sin. So called learned Brahmin had finally been enlightened by a meat seller.

Arjun, among the most fortunate one had God incarnate as his counsellor. What did the counsellor cum teacher, friend philosopher guide say? "You lack wisdom – Sankhya" After all he was the Godhead.

His basic premises based on sensory date and instinctive demand conditioned by emotions of love and hatred was erroneous. Therefore, the need for imparting Sankhya – the wisdom of life in all its totality. Sankhya is all about the Purusha – not a male person but consciousness principle. A fundamental all inclusive principle outside of which nothing exists. Sankhya as a philosophical school divides reality into two faces. One the subjective consciousness which is imperceptible, the other perceptible objective face –Prakriti or nature.

The objective perceptible face can easily be accessed by the sense organs, grasped by the mind and analyzed by the intellect. Senses, mind and intellect finite in their capacity cannot understand the intricate laws of nature and thereby the mystique of consciousness. The whole domain of consciousness except for that which governs our waking state and to a certain extent our dream world continues to remain in the domain of occult –a mystique unraveled.

No wonder Penrose the great physicist, Nobel Laureate stressed the need for a new science to explain mind and consciousness. Arguing about the non –computability of consciousness, he says that conscious thinking involves ingredients that cannot even be simulated, leave alone computation. Mind must indeed be something which cannot be described in any kind of computational terms. He argues strongly for a fundamental change in the quantum mechanical world view.

The boundary between physics and metaphysics was being obliterated.

This is what Lord Krishna's discourse was all about, elevating his disciple's psycho -physical consciousness to the spiritual level where physics and metaphysics were the same. Integration of consciousness is where the identity or existence coalesced with consciousness leading to blissful state of infinite knowledge. Satyam Gyanam Anantam Brahma. Absolute is the ultimate truth -knowledge infinite.

Lord Krishna starts with the idea of Sankhya – a knowledge of the universe as 'it is in itself'. Once the cosmic structure with its subtleties is understood, then yoga becomes the way of life. Yoga – how to act in a totally impersonal manner. That is what ego -less detachment or Vairagya is.

We are all individualized units of a cosmic society, but only identifying ourselves with a limited human social organization. We compromise on our ego centric behaviour to extent that we continue as the members of the society in a hassle free manner. Nothing belong to us, but our ego tells us otherwise. Our physical body is an aggregate of five elements which on death revert back to their source. Mind is a product of rarefied subtle elements, Tanmatras, sense organs belong to their presiding deities, like sun, moon, fire etc. It is a totally borrowed existence. Death then becomes just a change of worn out clothes.

Particular Individual being a unit and a part of the universal, living a borrowed existence was dependent on the universal. Physical Nature provided us air to breathe with necessary oxygen to survive. It provided us food to nourish and water. All resources for survival came from nature. We in our inflated ego consider ourselves as the masters of the universe. We expect nature to play second fiddle to us. Ignoramus –that is what you are, Krishna told Arjuna and not so subtly. Do I have a way out? Yes certainly you have, but not by the kind of escapist mentality which you are displaying. Uttishtha Kaunteya. Awake and arise. It's a win win situation. If you die in a battle fighting for the cause of righteousness you will be welcomed in heaven, and if you win and survive the entire kingdom is yours to enjoy. A very sound management principle.

However all action has to be by way of duty without any attachment to the fruits thereof. Since all the components of our psycho-physical individuality belong to the cosmic forces and consciousness is involved in space and time inaction is impossible. Action is a movement, unavoidable because of space and time. Duty or Swadharma is action guided by the spirit, not the mind or intellect. It does not follow the logic of the intellect. It's supra rational or supra logical.

The result, outcome or fruit of an action is always in future. The idea of futurity is an involvement in time, hence it is not duty. Duty is a sense of transcending space and time.

The most interesting law of nature is the law of gravitation. It is a great benefactor as well as a great obstacle. It does not permit me to fly or walk on water but gives me a limited permission to lift my leg and walk. It operates on all things material because there is a quantity, a quantum.

Spirit is quantum less so not subject to law of gravity. It is the law itself. The whole discourse of Gita is to align one's self with the overarching law of righteousness and then the knowledge by identity so you become the source of the law and friend of law. Dharma –the cosmic law is the law of integration –what keeps the society intact. Love is the rule. Mutual attraction, infinite outside summoning the infinite within is the law of gravitation. It has to be understood in that sense. Metaphysics of gravity.

Chapter - 16

KANT

He was short about five feet in height frail in physique; the scot from Konigsberg in Germany lived eighty years. One of his biographers writing about his routine said "Rising, coffee-drinking, writing, lecturing, dining, walking, each had its time." He overcame his frailty of physique by reliance 'on the power of mind to master the feeling of illness by the force of resolution', whenever he went for a walk in the afternoon, he would breathe only through his nose and would not talk to anybody. Better silence than cold. The man with a brilliant mind proved that you don't have to be tall and endowed with muscular strength to cause a revolution in philosophy. It is the mind and intellect which works. This was Immanuel Kant, who dominated the philosophical thought of the nineteenth century, with his Idealism and Transcendental Esthetic. So much so that Schopenhauer said that any man was a child unless he understood Kant. Another wise man said that there had been only three philosophers in the world, Plato, Kant and Acharya Shankara.

He was born at a time when Irish Bishop Berkeley had refuted materialism only to be confronted by a sceptic Scotch David Hume, who demolished the mind as well as the orthodox religion and proposed to destroy science by dissolving the concept of natural law. The onerous task of rescuing science and religious faith fell upon the physically short statured German philosopher, whom Hume had woken up from 'dogmatic slumber'. He felt it was his duty to save religion from reason and to save science from skepticism – a philosophy which could write the ideas of Berkley who held that matter does not exist, with Hume who said that mind does not exist. Partly influenced by Rousseau who felt that culture corrupts and a thinking man is a 'depraved animal' he became the torch bearer of the Copernican revolution in the Western philosophy and laid the foundation of modern critical philosophy and an altogether new attitude to the nature of truth. It was the beginning of the era of German Idealists and the 'Transcendental Esthetic'.

Anna questioned about the relevance of Kant in the context of Yoga and Vedanta.

'That is what I am coming to,' replied Rohit. Immanuel Kant authored his 'Groundwork of the Metaphysics of Morals' where he came out with the idea of 'categorical imperative – based on the supreme principle of morality as different from the 'Hypothetical imperative'.

When he says that an action as duty derives its moral worth not in the purpose attached to it, but in the maxim in accordance with which it is decided upon. A maxim of an action is it's principle of volition. Moral worth of an action depends not on its consequences, intended or real, but on the principle acted upon. Duty is necessity of action from respect for law. Law is the universal law – impartial applicable to one and all.

Kant went much beyond the idea of morality and duty. He realised our capacity limitation and stated that sense perception and thought cannot approach reality. He differentiated between the phenomenal world as it appears to our senses and the thing in itself the 'noumenal', beyond the reach of our reason.

We can only sense the forms and relate it to names. Mind can work only in terms of categories of quantity, quality, relation and modality or condition. A non – physical entity quantum less, devoid of any quality relation less unconditioned cannot be approached by mind and intellect. So the Reality or Truth though it exists cannot be known.

Now let me go back a few thousand years and the location shifts from Konigsberg in Prussia to battleground of Kurukshetra in India.

Categorical Imperative becomes 'Nishkama Karma' – action as duty without any regard to the outcome based on 'Swadharma', the universal law of righteousness. Hypothetical Imperative was termed as 'Kamya Karma' or 'Naimittik Karma', where an action is performed to ensure a desirable outcome.

Gita lays down the concepts of one's own duty 'Swadharma'. Here, there is no desire for outcome, because desire leads to anger, it is like an insatiable fire which veiling the mind is like the constant enemy of the wise, the greatest obstacle on the path of wisdom and knowledge.

But the second part about the categories of understanding is more interesting. While Kant acknowledges the 'noumenal' the Truth yet puts it beyond our reach.

But Lord incarnate Krishna does not think that way. Omniscient as he is, he has a methodology to approach the ultimate reality. Revealing the highest secret, sovereign knowledge, combined with experience, the sovereign profundity, the best sanctifier is directly realisable. It is based on righteousness, easy to practice and imperishable.

Lord tells his disciple that there is no limit to his divine manifestations. Whatever is endowed with majesty or prosperity is part of His power.

The whole creation is sustained only by part of himself.

Arjuna, the human representative is extremely eager to see the divine cosmic form of the Lord as 'All inclusive Absolute', which also symbolized the infinite time.

Lo and behold, here emanate the immanent forms flowing out of the transcendental universal.

'Behold, O Partha, forms of Me, in hundreds and thousands, of various colours and shapes, which include twelve Adityas, eight Vasus, the eleven Rudras, two Ashwins (Horseman Twins) and forty nine Maruts in seven groups of seven each, besides other gods. Lord, introduces the transcendental principle by stating that the entire world with the moving and the non – moving exist within his body and can be seen apart from whatever Arjuna desires to see.

But then comes a caveat. The limitations of the categories of understating. A limited sensory and mental spectrum. The divine form cannot be seen by human eyes. A divine vision is granted to Arjuna. He had to contemplate on the cosmic form by supernatural eyes because the Transcendental cannot be beheld by sense organs, mind and by intellectual comprehension. It professes the concepts of 'Aparoksh Anubhuti' – a direct apprehension by way of intuitive wisdom. It truly is the transcendental unity of apperception.

Endowed with the divine vision, Arjuna with his third eye could visualise the cosmic form, the radiance of the exalted one like the effulgence of a thousand Suns simultaneously blazing forth in the sky. Arjun saw in the body of God of gods the whole diversity differentiated universe as existing at the same place.

There is this interesting concept of 'God of gods'. So the group of gods needs an explanation.

The first among the group of gods mentioned are the Adityas –sons of Aditi – who symbolizes divine nature in the form of space and earth. She also is 'Muktirupa' – a symbol of liberation, a release from sins. The number of Adityas starting from seven goes up to twelve. Corresponding to each month of the year they represent the twelve forces of sun. Each Adityas is a sun in a different mode in each month. They represent time by way of transient nature of things including life. With each passing day, month and year the life gets shorter. The sun nourishes as well as withdraws the lives of things.

There is another explanation of twelve suns representing concentric circle of solar manifestation or energies. It is theological, astronomical and mystical. One is the sun around which earth revolves. It is our solar system. This solar system itself becomes a planet which revolves around a sun which is superior to it. The hierarchy goes on till the twelfth sun, which is the sustainer God Vishnu –all energy, total brilliance.

Now the other group called Vasus. Vasa is the abode in which something abides. Fire, earth, air, space sun, heaven, moon and stars form a group of eight deities. They symbolize the constituent principles of all bodies.

Now we come to the terrible ones the eleven Rudras. Trayambaka – the three eyed ones and Jalash bheshaj – those with medicinal powers. They have also been classified as the apotropaic deities which have the power to avert the evil influences. They are the deities of Antariksha – the mid region. Fierce, warrior like representing a thunderstorm with lightening who in the course of time become holders of the trident. They are the howler or red one as Prana, the one's which make you cry, because "verily the vital breaths are the cause of tears, because on departing they cause everyone to lament in tears".

No wonder, Rudras are the most complex deities, emerging out of Rigveda Samhita which in course of time in combination with various other gods became synonymous with Lord Shiva in his terrible form. Originally conceptualized as the fertility gods of a pastoral society, the ten senses and the mind make eleven Rudras. They thus become the controller of the human system.

Rudra as Prana – Vayu – the vital life breath, the principle of life is also intermediary between physical elements and intellect. Ten vital energies plus Aatma, Rudra the howler in course of time become Shiva – the benign god of multiple modes. Glories, peaceful radiating love and compassion included in the cosmic divine form are Ashwins and Maruts.

Ashwins the inseparable 'horsemen twins' are again the luminous deities of the solar family. One is supposed to be the child of night and the other the child of dawn.

They are the divine physician, both for gods and human. They are a combination of morning and evening stars. They are also the protectors of conjugal love and life, and always help the oppressed in distress.

Then the cosmic form contained the powerful storm gods known as Maruts children of Rudras born out of oceanic waters.

They represent the deified version of the great storms. They come from a far, from the seat of Rta, the regulating principle or order of the universe. Powerful and destructive, they can also be kind and beneficent. They assist Indra the king of gods in his battle who also is symbolized as eldest of the Maruts. They have the power and strength to make the earth tremble. They are at the same time bearers of milk, honey and clarified butter.

Seeing all these gods in the cosmic form which then becomes terrible in the sense that it has large fiery eyes, frightening teeth resembling the fire of dissolution. All the warriors kings entering the mouth and their heads being crushed and reduced to powder Arjun gets totally petrified and extremely distressed. It is just an indication that the cosmic form of God is not easy to behold unless the person has attained a level of spirituality mature enough to discern. Scared, stupefied, bewildered Arjun requests the lord to revert back to his earlier form, wearing a crown, wielding a mace and holding a disc at hand. According to his request the Lord reverts back to his non – terrible form.

The whole idea is that it is extremely difficult for the humans to comprehend the cosmic form of the Absolute. It requires single minded devotion, by getting rid of nescience or ignorance. One has to be devoid of all attachments to objects and free from enmity towards all beings. It is the gospel of love supreme.

It is the breaking of the barrier of limited consciousness that constitutes the movement towards perfection.

Chapter - 17

KANT REVISITED

A little description about Kant, his life style and philosophy today. Kant as a philosopher of transcendental idealism, may have been a stickler for time when his evening walk was concerned, was fond of good things of life according to his biographers. While for Hegel 'eine gutes bier' was the drink, Kant preferred canary wine to lager lout. Maybe the Scottish genes or he felt wine was better for socializing, yet Patrick Cannon to explain his metaphysics has to send him to a bar and drink beer, on a Friday night.

Kant along with a friend went to the bar maid and said 'Two Beers please'. 'Your ID's please' replied the bar maid. She looked at the ID's and matched the 'state approved appearances' in the ID with their actual profiles, satisfied that they were of right age served them – with two glasses of the golden brew. The amber liquid tickles his mouth; there is a mild burn while he swallows it. You can hear sounds of billiard balls hitting each other because there's a game of pool in the next room. Music is playing in the juke box and everyone in the packed bar – room seems to be enjoying themselves.

Sitting at the bar enjoying a drink – Kant along with his friend, getting the glass after verification of his and friends identity is the ideal setting for explaining Kant's 'Transcendental Idealism'. The bar – maid examined the ID's, matched the photographs with their actual appearance and was satisfied that they were above twenty one years of age.

That was an informative portrayal of reality from the barmaid's point of view.

In 'The Critique of Pure Reason', the whole issue was whether the appearance reflects the reality. The answer was an emphatic 'No'. Appearance is phenomenon and reality is the ' thing in itself ' (ding-an-sich) the 'noumenon'.

The golden brew, the feeling of cold glass held in hand, the taste of beer, the smell of fermented Barley brewed with hops, the mahogany counter of the bar, were all sense experiences – a phenomenal experience, sensory, mental.

After you have had a few glasses, the 'psychological filter' goes haywire. Time starts moving a little faster. This again is a sense experience, the Beer effect termed as "temporal compression". With extra caffeine or amphetamines the time slows down – the 'temporal dilation'. So Kant was right in the sense that time was a relative concept – a subjective aspect of our experience.

You are waiting for your girl friend at a train station. Ten minutes appear like an hour. She arrives and you hit the nearest pub guzzling beer for more than an hour. It seems like ten minutes. So much for the appearances, the senses and the processes of mind. Two more experiences in the bar explain two of his principal concepts.

They go back to the bar counter asking for another two glasses of beer, the cans had not yet arrived at the scene, and bar –maid in a 'moment of inattention' drops a glass and it falls on the floor and gets smashed.

Heisenberg with his theory of uncertainty and indeterminacy had not yet arrived, so Newton's law of gravity and deterministic physics regarding motion ruled supreme. This smashed glass was therefore an explanation for causality, a cause effect relationship in Kant's categories of understanding, which were in accordance with reason. Kant was sure that given the rigours of law of gravity the glass was bound to fall down once it left the hands of bartender.

Third principal concept which Cannon explained by Kant's bar experience was an awareness of pressure of bar stool on which he was sitting, the weight of T-shirt on the shoulders, the music, the after taste of beer, the fragrance of perfume, fluorescent signs advertising alcohol brands – various senses experiences, touch, sound, taste, smell and sight – unite into a consistent whole which is Kant's 'transcendental unity of apperception'.

Kant stated the problem, provided partial solution and paved the way for further probe into the idea of 'Absolute' for Schelling and Hegel.

Kant almost came to the borderland of reality and then retraced his steps.

The 'Transcendence' was within the space time framework where knowledge was not so much occupied with the objects than with 'a priori concepts of objects'. Yet it was within the mental framework – the categories of thought.

In Gita the metaphysical dialogue is between Godhead and the human representative. The teacher philosopher could not have been sent to a bar, but one could easily evidence the idea of super sensuous intuition, the divine eye. Divine eye does not come instinctively. It involves tremendous effort and deep detachment. Sadhana – penance, an ascetic discipline, a whole soul effort with the power of discrimination, self – discipline and a deep aspiration. Viveka, Vairagya, Shama, Dama, Uparam, Titiksha, Shraddha and the grace of God.

Viveka is to get rid of nescience or Avidya, where a person is able to discriminate between what is eternal and what is transient. The noumenal as distinct from the phenomenal.

To get a super sensuous vision, involves a super sensuous effort. There is the story of a person by name of Madhava, brother of Acharya Sayana whose commentary on Vedas became the base for all further western literature on Veda, like those of Max Mueller and other Western indologists. Madhava like his brother was a very learned person. Madhava chanted Gayatri Mantra innumerable times during his Sadhana. He heard a voice that he will not have a 'vision in this life'. All his efforts gone waste, frustrated, he gave it all up and became a renunciate. Immediately divine voice asked him, 'Why all this chanting? What is it that you accept me to give you? Nothing said the poor man. It was told that I will not have a vision in this life. He was told that the moment he became a renunciate, it was a kind of rebirth and second life. Effort combined with deep detachment. The divinity asked him as to what he expected from the divine Lord. 'Nothing, absolutely nothing' was the reply. Lord said, 'if I appear then I can't leave without giving something. Since you have asked for nothing, you shall have everything'. Madhava, hence forth became Acharya Vidyaaranya – an omniscient person.

His years of penance, chanting yielded results, though a bit late. The story for whatever it is worth, has a lesson in it. His efforts God wards which is termed Yoga is a difficult and tortuous path, where inspite of efforts it may lead to temporary setback, frustration, yet the effort in the right direction never goes waste.

'Swalpmasya Dharmasya, Trayate Mahato Bhayat'. Even one step in the right direction, according to the universal law of righteousness – Dharma is the greatest saviour. There is no destruction of right action. It yields merit, which remains with you as an asset.

Gita also exhorts a human to make efforts to transcend the intellect. The sense organs are superior to the gross insentient limited body, but mind is superior to the sense organs. Intellect is superior to the mind, yet it has its own limitations. 'That' is superior to the intellect.

Human as a species are privileged to be endowed with intellect, the power of reasoning, beyond instincts. Intellect can go beyond ordinary sense perception. A power to ratiocinate with affinity towards sense objects is the lower one and limited. Yet we have a higher reason which enables us to have a premonition of higher existences. Mind to super mind, opening up a new vista of possibilities – freedom and immortality Lower self needs to the surrender to the higher one. Once the sovereignty of mind and intellect is overtaken by the sovereignty of the higher self – it is the plane of transcendental super consciousness.

There is a clear classification, a hierarchy where the subtlest is at the top. There is nothing superior to 'That'. That is what has 'Thatness' in it. Something inexplicable. 'I am what I am', was the answer of God to Moses. It goes beyond Tvam 'Thou' because 'That' appears as some entity though transcendent yet remote from a human point of view.

Difference between what appears as truth and what is intrinsic as truth, apparent and real has been brought out clearly in Gita without Lord Krishna and Arjun visiting the beer bar.

Lord Krishna was God incarnate. To understand God in a phenomenal world the symbol has to be a human appearance, just like any other person of the species. Arjun thinking him to be somewhat intellectually superior, not aware of his godliness found a matured teacher, friend philosopher and guide in him. A charioteer with multiple skills. Little did he realize that behind the serene face, the appearance was hidden the ocean of infinity.

There have been critics of Gita, who held a view that it provided a philosophical base for an autocratic system based on the hierarchical classification of society, wherein the hegemony of the ruling classes could not be questioned.

Even a battle involving violence was justified. A sinner also got absolved once he took refuge in God. Lord Krishna could grant deliverance to a sinner provided he surrendered to the concept of cosmic law of righteousness. This interpretation is based on physical meaning rather than the spiritual context. I will narrate the story of Valmiki, a robber turned a sage seer.

Chapter - 18

VALMIKI

The sage Narada wondering in all realms, was in one of his earthly sojourns was passing by a forest where he was accosted by a bandit called Ratnakar with the intention of robbing him. Whenever the bandit accosted someone, his very cruel expression made people cower in fear, ashen faced at the sight of impending death. Here was a person who did not show any signs of fear, totally unfazed. The bandit Ratnakara son of sage Prachetasa, who had turned to robbery because he had lost his way in a forest and was brought up by his foster father who was a hunter. Since Ratnakar had a large family, with too many mouths to feed, he took to banditry and starting robbing the travelers. Today was a day of surprise for him. Here was a person full of equanimity with no expression of fear. Instead, Narada questioned him as to why he led a life of sin robbing others committing violence. It is simple said 'Ratnakara – I have to feed my family'. Narada asked him to go and ask his family that the sin he commits by robbing, injuring and killing people, the proceeds of which are shared by the family to satisfy their hunger, would the family sharing the benefits also share the sin incurred by committing the crimes. He tied Narada to a tree and so that he couldn't escape and went back to his family. He asked each member of his family whether they were willing to share his sin. After all he was leading the life of a sinner and criminal because of his responsibility to feed them. None of them was willing to share the sins. It was his look out as to the path he followed and his responsibility to take care of his family. No sharing of burden of sins. It was an eye opener for him. He came back and fell at the feet of the sage and asked him to a path of salvation by way of repentance. Narada asked him to chant the name of Lord Rama. Seeped into sinful acts all this while, he could not chant the divine word. Narada said you chant in reverse 'Mara' – one who is dead. It was easier and years passed till one day Lord Brahma saw the bandit of the old times meditating so deeply that ants had covered his body with mud to build an anthill. He was blessed by the Lord creator and given the name of Valmiki – one covered by ant hill or 'Valmika'.

In course of time he was hailed as the Adi kavi the first poet in Sanskrit literature. A bird's death led to the epic Valmiki's Ramayana. Early morning he was heading toward River Tamasa for his morning bath, where two herons were in a mating mode, when a hunter's arrow struck the male, who was killed and fell on the earth. Overcome with grief he caused the hunter "Maa Nishad Pratishtha Twamgamah Shashwatih Samah, Yetkraunchamithunadekam Avadhih Kamamohitham" which meant that 'you hunter, you repent rest of your life and suffer, find no rest or fame, for you have killed an innocent unsuspecting bird of a loving crane couple'. It was the bereavement of the bird which led to the first verse or shloka, with multiple meanings. When he came to his ashram he analysed the verse, he found it was bound in four steps. Each stanza had eight syllables and it could be sung to the rhythm of a Veena – a string musical instrument. While he was discussing with his disciples, Lord creator Brahma appeared and told him that the divine inspiration to poetry came from the Lord himself, and he has to write the story of Lord Rama in similar verse and Ramayana – the great epic was the result.

This is mythology. What does it convey? There is no one who is born sinner. It's not in the genes. The circumstances make you a sinner and yet for sinner also the pathway to freedom is open. I again tend to agree with Weber here that Ramayana the epic is a poem in metaphors which conveys a change in value systems in the process of evolution from a chalco-lithic age to Iron Age. How poetry can have a divine source of inspiration brings me to another of my favorites. Aurbindo the philosopher says that the best of poetry originates at a superior level of consciousness, in the super mind, conveyed through mind and speech, and super mind or supra consciousness is closer to the divine.

What is sin and who is a sinner. I revert back to Gita. We discussed various interpretations.

"Sarva-Dharman parityajya mam ekam sharanam vraja, Aham tvam sarva-papebhyo mokshyishyami ma shuchah".

Abandoning all Dharmas, of the body, mind and intellect, take refuge in Me alone, I will liberate you from all sins, grieve not said LordKrishna.

"Gib das Ich auf (korperlich, geistig and intellektnell), suche Obdach mir in mir, ich will Dichvon allen Sunden befreinen kranke Dich nich", responded Anna. Wow that's great, we have the Deutsch expression as well.

Noblest stanza, yet the most controversial stanza of Gita, depending upon how it is interpreted.

For the philosopher Ramanuja it is the ultimate final verse, Charam Shloka of Gita and for a polymath cum historian with Marxist leaning it is primarily this verse along with a few others which denoted an abject surrender to the strong and powerful and prompted him to regard Gita as a scriptural source which could be used without violence to accepted Brahmin methodology, to draw inspiration and justification for social action in some way disagreeable to a branch of the ruling class upon whose mercy the Brahmins depended. To the Marxist historian it was a text that was trying to synthesize an array of glaring contradictions and could only be written at a certain period during which the competition over the surplus produced was no so intolerable as to result in class conflict. It must have been an era of plenty. Economic determines political thought as well as the philosophy of the age.

Let us see what the Vedanta philosophers have to say about the verse. Firstly there cannot be cherry picking about the verses. What message a text was supposed to convey according to an author, the best person to elaborate it will be author himself. Perhaps in varying moods and even he may also lose clarity in interpretation. However in the absence of the author the readers interpreters and commentators biases find their way, because saintly, virtuous or selfish, degenerate, intellectually deficient, everybody views the text from one's own perspective

First a selection of few verses in a text which has seven hundred verses is bound to lead to interpretational conundrum.

Is the verse in question – sixty sixth of Chapter XVIII, is an advise to a sinner, that he has a way out whereby he can be liberated from all his sins by taking refuge in the Lord. A total surrender after abandoning all Dharma's. Now what is sin and who is a sinner.

To Arjun's query as to why Lord Krishna propagating a doctrine of immortality of soul and yoga where by one has to follow a path of renunciation abandoning all desires, is being motivated to engage in violent terrible action of killing his own kinsmen, friends, teachers etc. in a battle -confusion worst confounded. Why does a person engage in sinful act. What is the impulse, the source of this evil? Once the intellect, right reason gets deluded, covered by the smoke screen of ignorance desire and anger, lead to sin. Ego-propelled desire to grab the object, dominate it, possess it, exploit it, and remove by force or violence anyone resisting it is the enemy – the Satan which is responsible for our deviant behaviour in causing war, disharmony and chaos, because it is not in harmony with Dharma –the righteous law of universe, the harmonious law of nature. Enemy number one – always present all around is desire seated in mind senses and intellect. The enemy within can be destroyed by knowledge and wisdom. Who is to be slain in the battle – the enemy within in form of desire, source of sin and evil to be purified by a faculty superior to intellect, an intuitive wisdom which can destroy the mighty armed foe. Where does social action, class distinctions figure in it?

Action guided by wisdom becomes sanctimonious. The prescription is that cut asunder the doubt of self born of ignorance by the sword of knowledge and take refuge in Yoga. Lord who seeks you to take refuge in Him is Yogeshvar. The ultimate destination of Yoga. So a sinner doesn't seek asylum in a war strategist Machiavellian charioteer, but in the infinite absolute – divine in it's glories.

The moment Valmiki realised that all his family members were happy sharing the booty which he collected but were not willing to share the karmic liability, the wisdom dawned and the sinner became a Brahmarshi highest among the sages.

Aurbindo when he says, truth – one and eternal, which we try to seek can be multifaceted, multi dimensional and therefore cannot be shut up in a single trenchant formula. It is not likely to be found in its entirety in any one philosophy or one scripture. Scripture have two elements local temporal, temporary pertaining to the ideas of the period and region in which it was produced, while the second part is the eternal imperishable universally valid for all ages and all countries. In the context of a scripture what is of permanent value is that which besides being universal has been experienced, lived and seen with a higher than intellectual vision. Among the various schools of Vedantic thought, each finds in the

Gita its own system of metaphysics and trend of religious thought, dualism, non-dualism, qualified non – dualism etc. We have to seek from the scriptures the actual living truth it contains, which will be suitable to the mentality and helpful to the spiritual needs of the present day humanity. Gita opens the door to our highest psychological possibilities.

Philosophy is a quest for truth – truth inviolable. Mirages of metaphysics yield water to the wise, once the illusion disappears and things get viewed in the light of divinity and eternity.

Chapter - 19

PRAJAPATI

Prajapati, the Lord Creator, loudly proclaimed in an open celestial assembly that *aatma* is free from the every kind of evil, does not decay with age and is immortal. No hunger, no thirst, no pain, no sorrow or grief, such is the great *aatma* which is to be known. Gods as well as demons, both heard it. The gods sent their king Indra and demons their King Virochana to the Lord creator to fully understand the concept so that once they knew *aatma* they would gain mastery over all the worlds. Both stayed as humble disciples for thirty-two years practicing austerities, controlling their senses and leading a very disciplined life. Lord creator was impressed by their austerities and sacrifice of pleasures of the physical world, asked them the purpose of their visit. Both said that they had come in search of knowledge of *aatma*. In a rather enigmatic statement, Lord said," That *Purusha*, the being which you see in your eye is the aatma — immortal fearless Absolute." On further query regarding reflection in the eye, Lord replied, "It is reflected everywhere including water? Please go and see your reflection in water and discover it. We see ourselves, reflection in totality, including hair, nails etc. This is the *atma.*

Having been told the concept of *atma*, both started heading home. Virochana saw his reflection in water, saw an image of body and happily went home and told his fellow demons that this body is *atma.* Let us look after it, protect it with all efforts and then began the celebrations. Indra, the king of gods, wiser than his demon counterpart started entertaining doubts about it. How could a perishable mortal frame like body be identified with immortal self? He, instead of going home, took a u-turn and was at Lord Creator's feet, expressing his doubts. "Another thirty-two years of austere disciplined life here and you will get your answer", said Prajapati. After having completed the second term of discipline lasting thirty-two years; Indra was introduced to a greater reality than the physical body. The reflection of the waking state is body; it is what you see in the state of dream in the *atma*. Somewhat satisfied that the new statement went beyond pure physicality, Indra started heading home. Halfway through, the doubts reappeared. Dream world is a makeshift world, which collapses once the person wakes up. He retraced his steps and stood before Prajapati in humble submission expressing his doubts, back to another term of austerities of thirty-two years. This time it was neither the physical body, nor the one conditioned by the sorrows of dreams, it was what you experience in deep sleep state is the immortal fearless *atma*. The deep sleep state is a state free from all worries, all obligations, a state of bliss. Satisfied for the time being, Indra headed home, but the doubts would not spare him. It was a state of joy, quite alright, but you were lying unconscious, consciously aware of it later on, when you got up fresh saying 'I had a good night's sleep.' There was something definitely amiss. About turn and back to square one. Thank god, this time the confinement was only for five years. Expecting another disciplined term of thirty-two years, Indra was extremely relieved when told that the discipline was to last for only five years. Relativity of time explained. Having completed one hundred and one years of intense austerities the hardcore aspirant was now entitled to be instructed about the final truth Body physical or mind psychical are conditional by space–time and characterized by finititude, a consciousness of its limitations as well as there being something beyond it. *Atma* is bodiless, nameless, formless, truth, unthinkable, invisible. It is allegorically supreme luminosity — perfection, so as to say. Impersonal supreme person. It is not a contradiction, just a way to describe the indescribable. It moves the fastest, it moves not. It is the transcendent principle, the quantum less silence of *Aum*. The eye of the eye, the ear of the ear. There is a sequel to this story, not in a chronological but logical sense. Indra had already learned the secret of the self. Although both being progeny of the Lord Creator, gods and demons have always been engaged in a battle against each other according to mythology. The only difference is that demonical *Rawana* in *Ramayana* is replaced by unjust evil cousins in *Mahabharata*.

Brahman, the Eternal Absolute has always been on the side of gods, the followers of the path of righteousness, like Lord Krishna being the charioteer of Arjuna — the warrior fighting for a righteous cause. Gods having defeated the demons, puffed up with their ego, celebrated their victory which they considered to be an outcome of their valour, strength and courage. Eternal realizing that their ego needs to be deflated, wanted to teach them a lesson. It was reported to Indra, the king of gods, that a strange demon like creature was sitting on a tree close by. Fire god, Agni, was sent to investigate. The *yaksha*, tree creature, asked Agni to introduce himself. Full of vanity, Agni said, "It appears that you are not aware of my power. I can burn and reduce to ashes all that exists in the worlds." Not impressed, Yaksha put a blade of grass in front of him and asked him to burn it. Fire god with all his might, could not burn it. Humiliated, his head hanging down in shame, he came back and reported to his king that he was not able to identify the creature. Rest of the story, he withheld. Then Vayu, the powerful wind god, was sent to identify the stranger. Proud of his strength, Vayu on approaching the tree told Yaksha sitting on it that he had the power and strength to blow away all that exists in the world. Again, a blade of grass was put in front to him to be blown away. However hard he tried, he found impossible to move it at all. It remained kind of glued to the earth. Humiliated, with face down, he came back and confessed his inability to discern the stranger.

The king now had to step in and therefore took upon himself the task of identifying the stranger. Instead of meeting the strange tree person, he met goddess Uma, daughter of snowy Himalayan Mountains and asked her, "Who incidentally is the strange creature perched on the tree?" "*Brahman*, the eternal Absolute", replied Uma. He immediately understood. His one hundred and one years of austerities, penance and self-discipline had paid off, because among the gods he was nearest to 'That'. 'That' is the eyeless which sees everything, earless which hears everything, without air who breathes, mindless who thinks and understands everything. All the powers of the organs and their presiding deities are derived from this one source.

Two simple lessons from the story, it is not easy to understand the concept of *atma*. Even the king of gods had to spend more than hundred years sacrificing all the pleasures of living, living in austerity and discipline to gain the knowledge of the transcendent and it needs a tremendous degree of epistemic curiosity to prove your eligibility to the divine teacher before he finally teaches the truth to you. *Abhyasa* — constant effort and *Vairagya* — deep detachment for stilling the mind before it gets upgraded.

A slightly complicated definition of *atma* is that which is distinct from the body — gross, subtle and causal. It is beyond the five sheaths *panchakosha*, denoting different levels of experience — physical, psychical and intellectual. It is witness to the three levels of consciousness in waking, dream and deep sleep state. It is existence, consciousness and bliss infinite. The gross body primarily consists of cells — an agglomeration of certain elements like carbon, calcium, phosphors etc. and water, energized by air fire, that is the breath and food intake, with intercellular large spaces. It is fully dependent on all its constituents for its functioning and relies on the Mother Nature to provide resources like water, air and food for its sustenance. Any element deserting it, it dies and gets decomposed. The first negation is that *atma* cannot be identified with a perishable body.

The great adventure of Indian thought is that in psychological terms it broadly professes four states of consciousness. The waking state where body, mind, senses all operate; dream, a mystery — body and senses at rest, mind creating its own world; sleep a super mystery; and thereafter 'I' and the 'Universe' the greatest mystery. *Atma* neither wakes up, nor does it dream, and does not sleep. Even in deep sleep we exist not an 'annihilated nothing', but in totality of quietitude. *Atma* becomes the constant factor in all three states.

In India even now to a large extent, marriage is a sacrament, rather than a contractual obligation. Philosophy in the ancient times was wedded to psychology, so the relationship continues as far as old philosophy is concerned. In the West, psychology found a younger, apparently handsome, spouse called science and divorced philosophy to tie the knot with the youngster. Perhaps one has to find a new relationship whereas the best in philosophy and best in science is incorporated in psychology and any linkage with the domain of the esoteric may not be treated as a pseudoscience from a psychological perspective. Para psychology, Psi or transpersonal psychology stand on an equal footing with the other so-called scientific aspects of psychology. A happy triad of philosophy, science and psychology embracing life in its empirical phenomenal rational mode as well its working in trans-empirical mode would be presenting a total picture, each complementing the other rather than contradiction. Yoga of various disciplines.

Chapter - 20

DAWN

'Dawn' says the Rishi is the head of horse sacrificial. The sun his eye, wind his breath, his wide open month is fire-universal energy, Agni Vaishwanara. The time process in terms of a year which includes segmentation in terms of months and past present and future is his body. Heaven above is his back, atmosphere his belly, earth is his footing, the quarters are his flanks, intermediate quarters his ribs, seasons are the limbs of his body. Months and half months are their joints, the days and nights are that on which he stands, the stars are his bones and the sky is the flesh of his body. The sand is the half-digested food in his belly, rivers his veins and arteries, mountains his liver and lungs, trees, plants and shrubs hair of the body. The rising day is his front portion and setting day is his hinder portion. When he stretches himself, then it is lightening, when he shakes himself it thunders and when he passes water it rains. The sound that it makes neighing is the 'principle of speech'. Day was the grandeur that was born before the horse as he galloped; the eastern ocean gave it the birth. Night was the grandeur that was born in his rear and its birth was in the western waters. These were the grandeurs that arose to being on either side of the horses. He became 'Haya' and carried the gods, 'Vaji' and bore the Gandharvas, Arvan and bore the Titans, Ashwa and carried the humans. The sea was his brother and sea his birthplace.

The Upanishad of the Great Forest, Brihad Aryanak the most obscure and the profoundest according to Aurbindo, begins with the 'grandiose abruptness in an impetuous figure of the Horse of the Ashwamedh- the sacrificial horse which portrays the cosmos or universe as a symbol. "Full of gigantic imagery "entirely symbolic and highly complex to be conceptualized.

Egyptian hieroglyphs were a rather complex system, of writing, figurative, symbolic and phonetic all at once, in the same text. It was not until the Napoleons troops in 1799 during Egyptian campaign discovered the Rosetta Stone which had hieroglyphic and demotic scripts along with a text in parallel in Greek translation. This is when it became easy to decipher the hieroglyphics.

The imagery, the metaphor, the allegory and the symbols present a much more difficult challenge of deciphering because a Mantra is the manifestation of a thought process, which involves divinity.

It constitutes a mystical revelation in a language Old or Vedic Sanskrit, which is supposed to be learnt by sitting beside a master-the Guru, dispeller of darkness of ignorance by the light of wisdom.

As Aurbindo Says-

Profound subtle, extraordinarily rich in its rare philosophical suggestion and delicate psychology, the ideas like hieroglyphs were couched in a highly figurative and symbolic language. It would have been easy reading and understanding for the author's contemporaries who must have been accustomed to this suggestive dialect. However, for a modern scholar the method of the old has to be followed – 'to listen in soul to the old voices and allow the Sruti in the soul to respond, to vibrate first obscurely in answer to the Vedantic hymn of knowledge, to give the response, the echo and last to let that response gain in clarity, intensity and fullness.'

The provisional conclusions drawn on the basis of philology have to be very carefully scrutinized in the light of the images of the parable. Even more complex are the subsequent hymns.

Originally nothing existed. Everything enveloped by a hungry devouring, all consuming death. The hungry death contemplated to have a mind. Out of the intercourse between mind and speech was born the time process Non-sensical gibberish of a shepherd community or the profoundest of the philosophies if, properly interpreted and understood.

For interpretation of such complex subtle thought, historical context, modern science along with comparative philology, and an intuitive sense to capture the spirit is very significant 'Zusammenhang' which gives a comprehensive view.

It ultimately is knowledge by identity. The intuitive sense goes beyond 'scholarship and intellectual inference'. The first person experience, esoteric in terms of subjective consciousness cannot fully be explained in exoteric empirical terms except by way of symbols and metaphors. Many of the scientist, physicists or evolutionary biologists, those believing in chemistry have discarded various mythological stories regarding creation. There has been an effort to explain the 'big crunch' and universe emerging out of 'big bang' on the basis of laws of gravity. Newton was first to postulate the laws of gravitation. The force of attraction being proportional to the mass.

How do we postulate gravity for a mass less quantum less non-physicality? Leaving alone metaphysics for a while attraction and repulsion in the psychological domain remains out of fold of gravity. The whole immersive debate of consciousness, its root and implication arises out of it.

Sacrificial Horse represents the universe and subsequent hymn explain the cosmological process.

Esoteric process is being explained by taking recourse to the prevalent exoteric ritual of sacrifice.

Veda which is denotive of knowledge has been termed as vid sattayam, knowledge of existence, Vid vicharne, knowledge of thought, Vid lrilabha, the worldly affairs and Vid chetna Akhyan, consciousness. To understand such wide domain of knowledge, mere texts with normal etymological sense was not sufficient. Vedas as their essential limbs had phonetics, meter, grammar, Nirukta or glossary, and astrology which started with astronomy. It was inclusive rather than exclusive.

The concept of Horse becomes the concept of universe. Hungry devouring death meant darkness because there was no light of sensory perception. Hunger is a cosmic principle of grasping the objects. Since no objects exist so it is hunger as such of death. It is still a unity which tends towards diversity.

The Horse of the World, who is the vehicle for all beings, celestial, earthly humans, and demons originates from the cosmic ocean. The waters of the cosmic ocean are not water in the conventional sense; it is the cosmic soul which includes the cosmic mind with its flowing energies, cosmic vitalizing forces or prana.

These are the waters of supra-material causality. The message garbled in a difficult phraseology is rather simple. Horse of the worlds that is material gets elevated to supra-material as cosmic consciousness. We the particularized individuals, mortal and limited emerge out of that consciousness are manifestations of a free and infinite reality and the causal principle becomes our guide, mentor and friend and we derive assistance in making us what we shall be. There is a presumption of an urge the 'Hunger' in the cosmic consciousness for involution the big crunch leading to matter inconscient or may be some rudimentary consciousness. These days the scientist also says that the electron has a mind of its own.

Creation is explained as a trifurcation, Adhyatma subjective consciousness, Adhibhuta, objective world and Adhidaiva, the divine connecting link.

Metaphysics and physics will continue to stay apart unless both of them come to an agreement on the definition of consciousness.

Subject which was united with the object in the integral cosmic consciousness got differentiated, un-manifested Infinite in gross manifestation becomes differentiated retaining a centripetal force aspiring for unity and a centrifugal force for grasping the finite objects. Infinitude versus finititude.

The desires arise out of this sense of finitude, because of gravitational pull of the infinite visavis the gravitational attraction of the finite objects. Here it is gravity redefined.

According to Einstein gravity causes distortion in space-time. Intellect distorts knowledge by dividing the unity of being into subjects and object.

This is what the whole story of Kathopnishad- the dialogue between a human cursed to death by his own father and Yama, the Lord of Death.

The fundamental Vedic dictum 'Ekam Sat VipraBahudha Vadanti'. The same truth is spoken by teachers in different languages and varying accents.

Kuhn talking of priority of paradigms narrates the story of an investigator who hoped to learn something about what scientists took the atomic theory to be, asked a distinguished physicist and an eminent chemist whether a single atom of Helium was or was not a molecule. Both answered without hesitation but the answers were different. For the chemist the atom of Helium was a molecule because it behaved like one with respect to kinetic theory of gases. For the physicist it was not a molecule because it displayed no molecular spectrum.

Who was right? Both were logical in their viewpoint and correct in their own way.

No wonder that Aurbindo said in the context of that truth one and eternal which we all seek cannot be captured in a single trenchant formula

In Science the 'Paradigms' kept on changing at a much faster rate in recent years. From Newtonian Absolutes and mechanics to Einstein relativity and Quantum Mechanics, from Aristotle to Roger Penrose, Stephen Hawking, Schroedinger, Heisenberg and host of others, from Darwin to Haeckel and proponents of a bio centric universe.

I had narrated the story of Nachiketa earlier. Once accompanying his mother to the cowpen he asked the mother as to why should we be reverent to cows and treat them like mothers. They provide milk to us like the mother she replied. You earn merit by worshipping the mother which takes you to heaven. How about giving an old cow to a poor friend. That would amount to cheating, said the mother. An old cow which doesn't yield any milk is not an asset but a liability to whom it is gifted and leads one to hell. It was his first lesson regarding the sacrificial ritual. This is why he objects to his father gifting old cows and is cursed to death.

He asked Yama the Lord of Death a strange question about the Great Beyond.

"There are two opinions about a person who dies. Some say something exists, others say nothing exists. What's the truth?"

There are two approaches to consciousness, one intrinsically good, other the transient pleasant. Good is difficult to obtain, pleasant easy to get. The wise one always chooses the good that lasts, while the dull soul is attracted by the pleasant. God is subtler than subtlety which logic cannot reach. I wish I could meet more questioners like you desirous of knowing the truth God realization is through spiritual yoga.

Now comes the interesting chariot analogy. Know the body as a chariot and soul as the master of the chariot. Reason the charioteer and mind holding the reins. Senses are the horses and object of the senses is the path. The path is absolutely fine and friendly till sense bellowing as wild horses distort the vision and chariot meets with an accident.

One following the approach of 'good' does not get distracted by the objects and senses are under control, can't run helter skelter, whereas those following the path of the pleasant are likely to go astray. Plato in his Dialogues followed the same analogy in Phaedrus and Socrates' dialogues. There were two winged horses pulling the chariot, one white the noble one taking it on the path of good and other black the ignoble one pursuing the path of pleasant.

Soul is the chariot riding towards the ridge of the heaven beyond which lies the knowledge, wisdom justice beauty etc. everlasting Truth and Absolute knowledge. The charioteer joins a procession of gods, led by Zeus, on his trip to the Heaven. Immortal white is able to soar above while Mortal Black has a very turbulent ride. The white with the soul wants to go higher towards the heaven, the black mortal pulls the chariot back to earth. Soul catching a glimpse of the heaven comes back to the earth. White winged horse was 'Thumos' imbued with a sense of spiritedness while the Black one had a passion for earthly possession. Chariot driven by reason with the aid of "Thumos" had to train the horses so as to move in harmony and reach the heavens. It was yoga Plato's style. The 'Path' is absolutely neutral, the objects present no problem, the problem lies with the senses which have to be directed properly, so as to takes you along the path of spirituality,while ego- directed sense make you follow the so called 'pleasant' path where the infinite within is in a devilish mode, leading to ultimate crash.

The teacher has to be very competent. Once the teacher is identified with the Absolute there is absolutely no room for any uncertainly or doubt. Since Atma is identical with ones own self then a self-realized person in his own guru.

That is why many of the great master say that it is almost impossible to find a perfect 'Guru' in the work a day world. The golden key is 'Intuitive Self identical consciousness' where 'I' is one with You and everything is an 'I'. There is nothing internal, nothing external 'I' as a subject merges with 'I' as an object.

Without mind, speech does not make known anything. 'My mind was absent therefore I did not perceive the world, without pragyan, the eye does not make known any form.' Subtler than the subtle atom like, larger than the largest, the self hides in the "secret" cave in the heart. When an individual strips himself of will and weans away from sorrow, then he beholds Him. Mind controlled and there by purified, in its sublime glory is able to comprehend the greatness of the 'Self-Being.' The self is not to be discovered or realized by 'eloquent teaching or hearing' but only by whom this being chooses and where Dhatu Prasad, -god's grace is there to lead you up the path.

Aristotle located the soul in the heart, Galen in the brain, Descartes in the pineal gland where the poet seer of Kathopnishad the curtain raiser for Gita located it in the heart. But this heart is not the physical organ pumping blood in the circulatory system. This non-physical invisible heart symbolizes the seat of soul all pervading. Everywhere at all times.

Beyond the senses are the rudiments of the objects, beyond the rudiments of the objects is the mind, beyond mind in the intellect, beyond intellect in the great self.

The subtler the nature higher it goes in the hierarchy. The gross is at the bottom. So, all yoga is an effort to move from gross to the subtle. The final world which comes from the teacher is Uttishta Jagrat Prapya Varannibodhat, Arise, awake and find out the best teacher and learn from him. The path of spirituality is as sharp as a razors edge, extremely difficult to traverse, so say the learned ones.

Here is the germ of yoga philosophy coming into direct contact with the divine consciousness by capacity up gradation from a mundane human level to spiritual super human level.

"Having taken the bow supplied by the Upanishads, the great weapon, and fixed in it the arrow sharpened by incessant meditation, and having drawn in the mind fixed on the Brahman, strike, o gentle youth that mark, the immortal Brahman".

It is to be targeted by Sravana-hearing, Manana-reflection and contemplation and then Nidhiadhyasana-meditation.

Yoga is, always has been and will continue to be a game of consciousness and evolutionary path where the final destination is 'cosmic consciousness'- the goal. The biggest challenge is to understand, consciousness, being 'conscious of consciousness'.

Existence, consciousness and bliss- I exist, I am aware of my existence, I am blissfully aware of my existence. The bliss symbolizes the infinite sense of existence consciousness eternal existence. At all times, everywhere.

A scientist leans towards physiology, the working of the neural system, superior frontal gyrus of the brain, neurons, synapses and ganglions, the psychologists starts probing the zones of conscious, subconscious and unconscious. The philosophers, Greeks, German Idealists the Cartesian Dualist the Realists, the Materialist each has his own views to offer. The ancient Indian philosopher psychologist, Rishi of yore with his mysticism, and intuitive philosophical bent of mind, goes beyond the unconscious to Turiya and

Turiyatita established psychological norms of consciousness to the states of supra-consciousness.

A biologist or a neuroscientist treats it as emergent of the brain and neural process, an epiphenomenon, unable to provide satisfactory answers to the problems of consciousness based on experimental methods, so is the case of psychologist and philosopher following an 'expositional method'. However whether we call it expositional text of first person subjective experience into a text as a third person data recounting the subjective experience presents the biggest problem.

Let me start with another interesting story about sage Yagyavalkya and Gargi, perhaps the only lady philosopher finding mention in the Upanishads. It is an irony of Indian social philosophical and knowledge traditions that in a land where river goddess Saraswati was treated as the goddess of knowledge, except for Gargi and Maitreyi very few women find mention in the principal Upanishads. A gender bias? No access to the gurukuls, the centers of learning. Gargi was an exception perhaps being the daughter of a sage a person fully conversant with knowledge scriptures. She was a born natural philosopher who had the courage to challenge. Yagyavalkhya in a debate. She was the first symbol of feminism in the Indian tradition.

There were two verbal encounters between all knowing sage Yagyavalkya and Gargi. In the first one she was somewhat overawed by the learned sage. Smarting under the insult, gathering her wits, prepared herself for a second round of intellectual sparring. Wise in her own domain she was not the one to throw the towel in the ring so easily.. She had to have satisfactory answers to her vexed questions of 'transcendent reality'.

Addressing the sage directly she said, '"I am going to shoot two questions,arrow like with sharp bamboo tips, once piercing the body will cause extreme pain and damage."

Undeterred the sage replied with total confidence 'Shoot Gargi', You are welcome'.

The first question read something like this. 'By what, O Yagyavalkya is that pervaded which is above the heaven, below the earth, which it is said is be identical with whatever is, with whatever was, and whatever will be', and is there a foundation or sub-stratum supporting space and time'.

It was a question about space, time and its transcendence in the Absolute Infinite. She confidently thought that she had put the sage in a real catch 22 situation, and questions will be unanswerable. Little did she realize the brilliance and knowledge of the sage.

It had along been held in Vedanta Philosophy that indeterminable infinite Absolute was indescribable in finite terms. It could be realized only through an intuitive Trans-empirical experience-a first person subjective experience.

If the sage did not answer the question he would lay himself to the charge of non-comprehension, and if he tried to describe the transcendental beyond space time in empirical terms he would be guilty of contradiction, misrepresentation and falsehood.

Unperturbed, the wisest sage in the gathering beaming with confidence uttered what would lay down the fundamental Upanishad principles of space time and beyond-consciousness, matter life, death and beyond.

'Avyakrita Akasa- 'un manifested ether, the subtlest of the subtle principle without a name form-nothing physical about it.

Gargi was satisfied with the answer, but came with a supplementary question. 'The un-manifested ether principle which is the sub-stratum of everything, space time and beyond-inconceivable must be having some foundation. I would like to have a description of this indescribable immutable homogenous substance. Metaphysical is to be described in physical terms.

Then comes a very interesting answer. 'There is nothing beyond the imperishable immaculate perfect Absolute. Neither gross nor subtle, neither long nor short, since it is not in space it is immeasurable, therefore dimensionless. It has no colour, neither darkness nor light, relation less. Neither space nor air water earth, non-elemental cannot be grasped through the senses of taste, sight, hearing, speech etc. It has no eyes, but sees everything, no ears but hears everything, no speech but speaks everything. It-has no mind but thinks everything. It doesn't breathe because it is energy itself. It has absolutely no measure of any kind, physical, sensory or psychological. Since it's beyond space time there is no inside or outside in it.

It does not consume anything nor is it consumed by anyone.

This was the 'mysterium tremendum et fascinans'- describable only in negative predicates. Neti Neti not this, not this. This is the supreme governing principle of the cosmos. It is neither objective nor subjective nor omnijective.

There is an order in the universe, governed by various laws of nature like the law of gravitation. The universal laws of nature, which have also been termed as 'Dharma' is logically perfect and emerges from the 'Para Brahman'- the perfect Absolute. This supreme sub-stratum of the universe is the inner controller, regulator the force, the fundamental cause of which universe governed by the laws in an effect.

From this linkage follows the principle idea of omniscience. Understanding the time process leads to predict future on the basis of past and present. Linking this to astronomical observations and planetary position has led to the science of astrology.

All material creation including life which energizes the matter is born out of the womb of hungry death and therefore what prevails in the physical nature is the law of hunger. This law has as its corollary the evolutionary principles of struggle for existence and survival of the fittest. Life in order to sustain itself depends on the body to gather its food and body an aggregate of certain elements is vitalized by life force is totally dependent on this prana for its survival.

So the final words of Yagyawalkya described the great wonder in terms of non-dependence and self existence, perfect autonomy of an all inclusive infinite.

Here Yagya becomes yoga. A transformation from a mentality dominated by the law of hunger to a law of love. Yagya then becomes a joyous sacrifice of interchange wherein an individual gives himself to others and receives others in exchange and finally individual surrender himself to the divine receives the universality of the divine as a recompense, from struggle of existence to total harmony of life.

Various philosophers have tried to provide answers depending on their predilections and thought process. Both Haeckel and Acharya Shankar base their solution on 'Monism', but with a fundamental difference. Haeckel solves the 'riddle of the universe' by recourse to a simple idea of 'Material Monism', based on Law of substance, a material substantiality of life, nature and universe. For Acharya Shankar it is spiritual monism, and Advaita relegates all things material to the lowest in the hierarchy of truth and nature and world becomes an illusory projection. Like a movement of actor in a movie on a cinema screen. Two extreme views both monistic with totally different paradigms.

Haeckel is easy to understand. Picking up the pen of Darwin, from where it fell, while treating theocratic ideas as irrational formulae of faith and clerical despotism; he demolishes anthropism and cosmological theory.

A human becomes the youngest and most perfect twig of the branch primates, who sprang from a series of manlike apes towards the end of the tertiary period. Man thus becomes a tiny grain of protoplasm in the perishable framework of organic nature. From 'Ape man' with no speech descends the speaking man.

The complete copulation of two sexual cell muscles marks the precise moment when not only the body, but also the 'soul' of the new stem cell makes its appearance.

Matter rules supreme and the myth of immortality of soul are destroyed. Why trouble oneself with 'the thing in itself,' whether the noumenal exists or not because we can do without it. You are born by a biological process, live life with experiences, good bad indifferent and finally bid goodbye to the world- period. Try to find out means to make life as comfortable, pleasurable as possible. Life is to be enjoyed to the full because there is no herein before and no herein after. No soul, no spirit. Everything comes to an end with life. Material monism, philosophical and practical and willy nilly most of us follow it, with a lip service to the spirit.

The other extreme is the Advaita Vedanta of Acharya Shankar. Just as Haeckel had picked up the pen of Darwin, Shankar the proponent of Advaita had picked up the pen of great idealist sage Yagyavalkya, with a gap of more than a few thousand years. Born in the Malabar region, on the western coast of Indian he was the disciple of Govindapada who had been a pupil of Gaudpada, author of Karika on Mandukya Upanishad and perhaps the first proponent of Asparsh Yoga- contact less yoga. Here was a youngster who at the same time asserted the importance of the orthodox faith and imbued with an untiring spirit of spiritual and religious reform.

On one hand was ritualistic tradition, exoteric in its approach which hardly catered to the spiritual needs of the people. Truth was being veiled by the theists by making an appeal to emotions and sentiments. The pleasures of heaven were the carrot dangled to people in return for sacrificial rituals in this world. Buddhism had a psychological appeal by addressing itself to the masses, but the denial of the soul left a void.

The void was filled by Shankar by his 'austere intellectualism' and subtle remorseless logic. so much so that is was remarked by one scholar that as all European thought is a footnote to Plato, so all Indian thought was a footnote to Shankara. While Yagyavalkya had propounded the doctrine of Atma, Shankar elaborated it by positing it as a fundamental concept from which everything else follows. It is the foundational principle to which everything else is consequential. It is beyond thought, because thought is a modification of mind belonging to the domain of non-self. It is a logical postulate which had to be taken for granted. The first principle from which flow different models. It was about the 'self-supreme', non-physical, non-empirical and the phenomenal world as an illusion. There is a clear cut distinction between matter and consciousness and matter is relegated to an inferior position, with consciousness reigning supreme.

Here Aurbindo interjects. Neither stark 'Material monism' nor extreme 'Spiritual Absolutism' by itself can be wholly satisfying. The truth lies somewhere between Haeckel and Shankar. The middle path which Lord Buddha tried to put forward but which again was left with certain inadequacies. Someday, some scholar philosopher will attempt a middle course which will supersede the two negations, the 'Denial of the Materialist' clinging to scientific positivism, realism and the 'Refusal of the ascetic' idealist's interpretation of Vedantic dictum of Ekmeva Advitiyam- 'one without a second'.

You seem to be rather enamoured of the master Aurobindo, why such a bias towards him among the many masters.

He was a revolutionary, one of the fiery leaders of Indian nationalist freedom movement.

He was the most unique and fascinating among the Indian philosophers and Yoga Gurus, with his own definition of Ashram in the classical Gurukul mode. It was the place where it was the teacher's privilege to lay down the rules of the ashram which all students had to comply with. They had no say in its operation.

From early childhood for fourteen years he lived in England totally divorced from the culture of his forefathers and developed foreign tastes and imbibed foreign culture. His is a unique case of de-nationalization and re-nationalization. In his studies for Indian civil service, he studied the six orthodox philosophies 'Shatdarshan' and was fascinated by the concept of 'Atman' in Advaita, yet he having qualified for the civil service refused to take the mandatory horse riding test because he did not want to be civil servant.

From the age of five to twenty years he only spoke English. This was the period where he had been is London school and king's college Cambridge, an atheist to agnostic to theistic, a liberal along with virtually a spiritual chauvinist, who interpreted Indian scriptures, Vedic Literature and Gita in an altogether new light. Here was a genius who found Schopenhauer to be more exciting than Hegel. He was a modern scholar philosopher who sincerely felt that it was wrong to weigh old happenings in the scale of modern ideals.

He was the unique one who appreciated that there were serious difficulties in Englishing a Hindi legend. As comfortable with Greek mythology as with the Indian he realized that the difference between Greek and Hindu temperament was while the former was vital, latter was supra vital. In Hindu mythology what is unfamiliar initially appears with a sense of roughness and bizarre is much more romantic and poetic in Greek. He claimed to be a yogi without renunciation in the conventional sense. Political activist became a religious recluse but contributed to the War effort for the British because England was a symbol of a progressive evolution towards democratic freedom whereas Nazism symbolized reactionary revolutionism.

He questioned everything and provided the answers. Could not the modern humanism and pacifism make it a reproach against the Pandavas the virtuous men brought about a huge slaughter that they might become the supreme rulers over numerous free and independent people of India. But at the time held the view that old happenings could not be weighed in the scale of modern ideals.

Sister Nivedita knew him as the one who believed in strength and worshipper of kali? Kali the force of Lord Shiva the destroyer. His transition from a revolutionary political activist to a yogi was a transition from Kali to Krishna Kali and Krishna finally.

His first realization of the vacant infinite was said to be while walking on the ridge of Takhti Suleiman in Kashmir.

The second was an awareness of living presence of Kali in a shrine in Chandod on the banks of Narmada River.

He was in the jail for political activities where the final realization dawned on him. He looked at the high prison walls, the tree in front of prison cell, the prison guard; everything appeared as Vasudeva, Lord Krishna. The prisoners in the jail, the thieves, murderers, swindlers all were Vasudeva. He found Narayan in these darkened souls and misused bodies. Krishna with the message of divine love had taken precedence over Kali.

When someone said that there 'There could be a god'. The response was that he refuses to believe that. I know that he exists and I know because I feel. An iconoclast who had the audacity to challenge the authority of Acharya Shankar though in a subtle manner. He was willing to undertake the 'hazardous task' of interpreting Vedic thought in contemporary terms. While writing a commentary on Brihadaranyaka Upanishad he was of the view that it would be an easy task to 'reproduce the thoughts and interpretations' of Shankar in an order terms and language. Any error would have been an error with so supreme an authority. But he thought that the demands of truth and spiritual need of the mankind demanded a new interpretation which could be at variance with the single side systematized by a medieval thinker. The great Shankar needs no modern praise and cannot be hurt by any modern disagreement. While acknowledging him as the first of metaphysical thinkers, the greatest genius in the history of philosophy was very relevant to a certain era, and a better method of interpreting truth would be to 'enter passively into the thoughts of the Old Rishis, allow their words to sink into our souls, mould them and create their own reverberations in a sympathetic responsible material'. This was knowledge by identity by following the intuitive methods.

A kind of 'Veda consciousness'.

He could view things critically to the extent of being irreverent. While acknowledging the contribution of Prof. Maxmueller on Vedic studies termed him as a grammarian and philologist rather than a sound Sanskrit scholar, one who construed the language well enough but could not feel the language and realize the spirit of it.

Chapter - 21

THAT THOU ART

Indian texts, social Philosophical mythological religious are full of sages and seers,the philosopher's of the Vedic era. One such sage was Uddalaka, whose son Svetaketu was not very keen on studies. Father sent him to a Gurukula, at 12 years of age and after completing studies for twelve years came back home at the age of twenty four having studied the Vedic Texts and scriptures,. Arrogant vain and full of himself puffed up with his learning. The father felt a little perturbed and wanted to teach him a lesson or two.

'Do you know, asked the father, that by knowing which everything is known, that by which unheard becomes heard, and unthought becomes thought and that which cannot be understood becomes understood.'

I am pretty sure that your learned teacher must have certainly imparted this knowledge to you. The vainglorious youngster was nonplussed, suddenly becoming somewhat aware of his ignorance., He was not willing to give up and utter nonsense he mumbled. Nobody had ever raised these silly questions yet he felt slightly humbled. 'But there is a sure way', said the father. It is possible that the knowledge of a single thing is the golden key to the entire storehouse of knowledge.

Ego diluted, somewhat puzzled, he was now paying attention to what his father said. Father gave him a clay pot to hold in his hands and asked him as to what he was touching. Obviously the pot he replied. Is it not clay that you are touching? He felt a little perplexed. The real substance was clay which could be moulded in any shape like a pot, a tumbler, and given different names. What exists is only clay, the substance, while all other names and forms are illusory, appearances as a result of your perception, something which the mind has created. All perception therefore is erroneous to the extent that it cannot discern between the substance and form. Variety, multiplicity is a product of mind, the reality is the essence, the substance which the mind is incapable of understanding.

Sensing that his son is keen on learning, he instructed him to get a little salt and put it in a cup of water. The boy followed the instructions. Father asked him the next morning to bring the vessel where he had mixed the salt in the water. Svetaketu discovered that the salt had disappeared. It appeared to be plain water. He expressed his inability to bring the salt, because it was not there in the water any more.

Father asked him to take a sip. It was salty. Father said that it is all there, on the surface, middle and bottom, yet it is invisible. It goes on to prove that things which are not apparently visible exist. The presence of salt is sensed not by eyes, but by the palate, not by vision but by taste. Similar is the case of 'Being', not discernible by the normal organs of perception and cognition because the universal is dissolved in each particular in a differentiated form. Why does it happen that way? Well, the limitation of the sensory and mental spectrum. Infra red and ultraviolet of the light spectrum are not visible. Capacity limitation of the eyes. The ears can only hear sounds within the audible frequency. We cannot see the micro waves but all the audio-visual programmes which entertain us on an idiot box are carried across the globe via satellite by them.

External instruments, a product of human ingenuity have their limitations being the creation of a limited mind.

This brings us to a very fundamental question; can we expand the capacity of the mind? Can mind be upgraded to a super mind? Yes say the scriptures, texts of Indian philosophy and psychology. In psychology of Yoga, mind can be trained in a manner which generates infinite capacity. If there a will there is a way.

Anna was keen to know as to where did the story come from? Any mythological texts? Well it is more a philosophical text, Chandogya Upanishad, author unknown, chronology uncertain, but what concerns us most is the content. These are not bedtime stories told by grandma to put children to sleep. One starts with a metaphor which is easily acceptable to the mind in a phenomenal mode, its limits of cognition. Salt dissolved in water it understands. Universal 'Being' present in all individualities sentient insentient beyond the ken of its ordinary cognition becomes debatable. No wonder we have orthodox philosophies of Being and Heterodox ones trashing it out right.

To the roving restless mind of an individual imbued with its intense wanderlust, its proclivity to probe and unearth all that exists on the earth, to fly to heavens to explore. All thing which it considers as external to it must be known. The only time it is at rest when a person is in deep sleep, a state of involuntary unconscious. It has to be trained, disciplined in a subtle manner, so none of the impression from outside is allowed to enter it. All things external get internalized.

Anna came out with a very interesting question? If everybody becomes a yogi what happens to this world? Well said Rohit, the ancients sages were no fools. They thought of these contingencies. The author of Gita, one of the prime texts of Yoga, ruled out the possibility altogether. Lord Krishna says that out of thousands of humans, some rare ones aspire to be Yogi and follow the path of renunciation. Out of those who follow the path of renunciates, some rare one becomes a yogi. So Yogi is the rarest of the rare.

Another answer is that of a Jivanmukta or 'liberated in life'. Let me introduce you to one of the rather under mentioned and understated characters in the Indian mythology, King Janaka of Videha, an epitome of 'liberated in life', a philosopher King, could have been Plato's delight. A king with boundless epistemic curiosity who was engaged in debates and discourses with the most learned sages and philosopher's of his time. Here in his case it was a psychological withdrawal from the work a day world.

Coming back to the clay and pot story and salt dissolved in water, aims to establish the 'Transcendent Absolute'. However the concept has to be gradually introduced. Starting with whole numbers the arithmetic begins with, addition, subtraction, multiplication and division takes us through to fractions, simple algebraic equation to more complex quadratic equations.

Upanishads, the philosophical part of Veda -the knowledge text professing Vedanta philosophy, the end or quintessence of Veda, incorporate stories where the teacher follows the technique of teaching like a good psychologist. It a gradual ascent of thought, step by step, fortified by logical arguments, at times appearing to be supra rational or super logical.

Here's another story. The same father son duo of Uddalaka and Svetaketu are characters of this dialogue well. It was all about food, something we can't live without, the basic need as Maslow would say. We all look forward keenly to our breakfast after the morning exercise, session. We find it difficult to sleep on a hungry stomach. A fast, intermittent or otherwise is okay for a while, but it does not obviate the necessity of food. All activity is directed to earn for a meal. What happens to the food that we consume? The food has three parts, subtle vibratory, not so subtle the middling part and gross matter. The subtlest part goes to form mind, the middling part forms the flesh and gross matter is thrown out of the body as excreta. Same is the case

with water we drink. The subtlest part goes to vitalize us through Prana, the middling part goes to blood formation and the gross part is excreted as urine. What about fats like clarified butter, oil etc.? asked the son. The subtle part forms our speech activated by the fiery element, fire the presiding deity of speech, middling part the marrow, and gross part the bone. Food water and energy sources are counter part of earth, water and fire element in nature. Thus the conclusion was that mind is made up of food, prana the vital force is made of water and speech by fire. Still the son appeared to be a little confused and sought further clarification.

Thus began, a very interesting practical experiment. Father advised the son to undertake a fast for fifteen days. No food was to be consumed, but he could drink as much water as he could. As long as he drank water, father assures that he is not going to die.

The boy did not eat anything for fifteen days, appeared somewhat emaciated before his father. 'Chant the Veda', said the father. The youngster expressed his inability. He was hardly able to speak. In a feeble tone he said, all the memory had vanished and mind was not functioning. Pitiable condition he was in. Please go and have your food, said the father. After having a meal to his heart's content, the speech become stronger and the mind with memory restored was back to its normal functioning. Water forming the Prana kept him alive all this while. What remained of fire was a tiny little spark, which if extinguished would have created a permanent loss of speech and mind, but meal restored both memory as well as speech. The fire started burning again.

The spiritual ascent, though still on an earthly plane was now becoming somewhat interesting and Svetaketu was getting more curious. Father had been successful in kindling the desire for knowledge. Here was an aspirant in making, after having passed the eligibility test of a fifteen day fast. The discourse was now shifted from mundane matter of food, water and fire to a somewhat higher level of consciousness of waking, dream and deep sleep state. Father asked the son to have a meal of choice and go to sleep. The son after a hearty meal slept like a log, and woke up fresh. It was 'Svapiti', which means sleeps.

'Sva' stand for one's own self or essential nature. In deep sleep, body and mind are at complete rest and it is only the consciousness which is present as quietitude, and a person is established in his own self, a condition quite different from the waking state where both body and mind are active, and dream state when body rests but the mind continues to be active. Similarly a healthy person is called 'Svastha', established in himself, disease free, totally at ease. In sleep you enter into your own self, withdrawn from all outside relationships. Tension free, worry free, no creditors, no mortgages, no liabilities. You wake up absolutely fresh and energized. In all other state than deep sleep mind is active in some activity, trying to interact and grab objects which it feels will lead to greater strength and satisfaction. In effect, you start losing energy which you had recuperated in your sleep. Since in any activity, physical or mental energy is spent, so food becomes a necessity, water liquefies the physical food, draws in the subtle part, provides energy and fire and gross parts thrown out of the system. After a while energy consumed water and food exhausted hunger starts knocking at the door again. Food getting absorbed in water, water in fire that is energy and energy dissipated in physical and mental activity you are back to square one. This explains, metaphorically the concept of life and death. All effects sooner or later get absorbed into a cause and final cause is called Sat or Satta Samanya, the generality of Being, the quintessential essence of everything. Once you understand the essence of a thing you know everything because it is the essential commonality of everything. So the initial question had been answered by recourse to metaphors, and analogies, we all have our roots in our Being, the universality within, which remains veiled because of nescience or our ignorance. We are always trying to retrieve our lost existence as universal all around and coming always a cropper.

Lo and behold, now comes the great sentence, 'O Svetaketu, ' Thou art That' 'repeated nine times because it doesn't seep in easily. An extremely difficult concept condensed into three words, could not be so easily understood. Wasn't the father being a little too optimistic in expecting a novitiate to Vedanta to understanding the meaning of the great sentence (Mahavakya). Its meaning was so deep and it connoted so much. Most of the great scholars are of the view that scripture Gita, the song Divine is a detailed exposition of the Great sentence. Out of eighteen Chapters of it's text, the first six correspond to Tvam(Thou), next six to Tat(That) and the last six explain the relationship and the whole text like the eighteen Chapters of Mahabharata are like the eighteen steps to perfection.

Extremely difficult to explain yet father spares no effort to make it understandable. Honeybees collect nectar and essence from flowers of different colours, fragrance and convert it into honey. Once honey is tasted it is near impossible to point the individual flower whose essence has been sucked by the bee. All individual nectars merge into the universal honey like all individual rivers merging into the ocean. Individual identity is lost, nay, it assumes a much larger dimension of universality. Explanations follow-a tiny little seed becomes a large tree.

Svetaketu, like any student finds it very difficult to understand the concept of real self –a loosely equated concept of Aatma. It is not an object with a form shape or size. Invisible, Imperceptible can only be explained by way of analogies and metaphors.

'You are that' But who you are? Well I am I. I have a name; I am a human, a body, a mind of my own, an individuality which differentiates me from you. Can you see your own eyes, your own self. No but I can't certainly be that. What kind of a riddle it is. By the way, what does it convey, stop fooling around with me and wasting my time. Obviously the first reaction and somewhat justified. Tomorrow you may turn around and say I and my brother or my parents, my friends they all are the same. What kind of a convoluted logic it is? Then I am not supposed to be skeptical. Nay, even the clothes I wear, tree in front of my house are all the same. Perhaps a normal reaction of a normal person.

There was a huge tree laden with fruits in front of the house where father son dialogue was going on. Father asked the son to fetch a fruit. The son ran outside, plucked a fruit and handed to his father. What do you see? It's obviously the fruit I plucked from the tree just now. Break it into pieces said the father. Well what do you see now? 'Small granules – tiny little seeds' said the son. What do you see inside the seed asked father. Nothing was the reply. It's so tiny that I can't see anything even if it be there. Uddalaka then said that inside is the essence which our naked eye is unable to see – atom, fundamental particle or just a vibration of energy. The huge tree bearing all those fruits containing hundreds of seeds is an effect of that invisible vibrant energy of the atomic subtle seed. That is the soul, invisible like salt in the water-Being.

Thus by dialogue was introduced the most inscrutable concept of Aatma loosely termed as self spirit or soul. The youngster a little while ago had protested that he could not be equated with anybody else. He had an identity of his own-his individuality. His body, his mental makeup, his behaviour, likes and dislikes were all different from someone else.

Even twins sharing the same womb and time of birth were dissimilar.

Here was the issue of ego-Ahankara, the differentiating factor, the self arrogating power of the four fold mind organ.

By introducing the concept of invisible essence in the seed, father had sown the seed of further enquiry in the mind of son. What is it that exists but cannot be seen, heard or thought of? The whole issue of Knowledge was now wide open.

The quest for knowledge has epistemic curiosity as it's starting point where Viveka, the capacity to discriminate between Sat real eternal existence and Asat the unreal transitory existence becomes all important.

Sruti says, self is real, Atma Satyam, rest is all Mithya or false. What constitutes the rest for an individual is his body mind etc. is termed false because it is not eternal. The body an aggregate of elements devoid of life forces decays and gets decomposed on death, mind disappears. What survives death, is the eternal self. It was this lost Being which the youngster was supposed to recover by way of self realization. So may ifs and buts. So subtle that it is invisible, imperceptible, unthinkable, yet the foundational principle of all experience physical as well as metaphysical.

The doyen of Indian Philosophy, of non-dualism in the Middle Ages, preceding Descartes by a few hundred years made a statement- 'Sarvo hi aatma astitvam pratyeti, naham asmiti'. Every person, including the most skeptics among the skeptics is conscious of his own existence and no one says that I don't exist. I exist therefore I see, I hear, I think.

It is a reality which forms the basis of thought. Thought is an effect which cannot find its cause just as our eyes can only see the objects outside in the space but is unable to see itself. What a pity? I cannot see my real 'I', my universal identity.

Svetaketu thought for a moment, that he was being led to a blind alley to search for an entity which was formless, dimensionless, quantum less, beyond all perception, beyond normal comprehension and empirical transactions transcending space time, and which could be indicated by a language of negative. Neti Neti. It is not this, it is not this.

We know about the body, its structure, anatomy by dissecting it. An organic whole, not a mere mechanical aggregation of cells, infused with a vital life principle. Gross enough to be investigated to the last minute details. It perishes with time because it consists of parts which remain unified by the life principle, and what is mortal is termed unreal.

One great philosopher in his graciousness seems to offer some hope when he says, it is different from gross, subtle and causal bodies, so all kind of bodies are ruled out.

The subtle causal body cannot be perceived, so anything beyond that becomes a near impossibility. It is beyond the five sheaths starting form Annamay Kosha to Anandamaya Kosha, five levels of experience starting form gross to subtle, a witness of three states of consciousness waking, dream and deep sleep. Beyond all five sheaths which are incapable of covering it. After all this negation there is a tentative definition that it is in nature of existence consciousness and bliss. Sat, Chit, Ananda which some philosophers interpret as Ananta infinite eternal therefore blissful. Existence makes me say 'I am', consciousness prompts me to say 'I am aware of my existence'. Eternal infinite am I – quintessential unity of consciousness, auspicious peaceful, non dual a transcendental state of consciousness where the entire phenomenal universe gets subsumed.

Chapter - 22

IMMORTALITY

Strong critics of Indian philosophy have always been saying that the Indian philosophy is simply a display of obsession with the idea of metempsychosis. It just has not been able to get over the irrational and silly ideas of rebirth and the law of Karma, it's genesis.

Let me narrate an interesting story from one of the largest Upanishads Brihadaranyaka the great forest of knowledge.

The preceptor in this interesting dialogue is a sage- one of the wisest of his times Yagyavalkya- name implying a person who knew everything about the law of sacrifice, the rituals, the procedure and the contents.

The sages of yore had their families as a householder. This one had two wives, Katyayni and Maitreyi. Mythology is interesting. Yagyavalkya paled into insignificance with regard to another sage Kashyapa who was supposed to have 21 wives, 13 of whom were daughters of Daksha- one of the progenitors in Hindu mythology. Without going into details of their family relationship, whether Yagyavalka's two wives symbolised his exoteric and esoteric aspects of personality, it was clear that Ashram Dharma as prescribed in ancient times permitted the sages to lead a householder life and have a family. Beyond a certain age was prescribed Vanaprastha which virtually meant leading a retired life after having fulfilled the family responsibilities. One started as a celibate student, then a householder and then a retired person with a sense of detachment and withdrawal from active life. Yet there was fourth order in the old age- sanyasa that of a renunciate. The sage thought it was time for him to enter the fourth order. He called both his wives and told them that he would like to divide all his property and worldly possessions equally between the two.

Katyayani worldly wise was thrilled, because henceforth she was going to be the sole owner of her share in the wealth, live the life on her own terms. Maitreyi who was daughter of a sage was made of a different stuff.

Herself, quite learned and wise, she asked her husband a rather simple question. 'Will all this wealth in my possession make me immortal?' 'No way' responded the husband-wealth and material possessions will make rest of your life a little comfortable but it can never be a pathway to immortality. She apprehensive of being deprived of the company of her loving husband said that all the property bequeathed to her had no meaning if it did not lead to immortality. She would rather keep company with her spouse, than claim the share in the wealth. However, she requested her husband who she knew to be amongst the most knowledgeable ones to enlighten her on the concept of the most vexed question of immortality.

The sage extremely pleased with the intelligent question and demeanour of his spouse was more than willing to satisfy her epistemic curiosity and thereafter began one of the most wonderful discourse on immortality.

It emphasises that death is not an end and nothing to be feared. It is just another kind of process which leads to training of the soul in it's march to perfection.

Every human being is potentially perfect free and infinite but existentially imperfect, limited and in a kind of bondage.

Having told his spouse even if she becomes the owner of entire earth and all it's wealth, it cannot make her perpetually happy because there is absolutely no possibility of being immortal by accumulating wealth. So he continues that he is going to let his spouse into one of the greatest secrets-namely the secret of immortality "Listen to me with rapt attention" is the command.

"Immortality is life eternal, and our work a day life is temporal-governed limited and conditioned by time. The eternal element is missing. We in the normal course of things in this world just cannot defy the law of time."

So is the case with property. All idea of ownership or possession is temporary and transient. A permanent possession is one which cannot be dispossessed. You may possess or not possess a thing, it has absolutely no linkage with the concept of immortality. Life in this world is conditioned by time and that is why we are all mortals. Even, our own body of which we claim to be the proud owners gets reduced to dust or ashes because beyond that there is no further reduction. Totally inconscient matter. That's why Lord Shiva the destroyer is potrayed as smeared with ash on his body.

The discourse after having trashed the idea of worldly possessions begins with the idea of love and attachment, attraction and repulsion and quest for freedom unlimited.

The biggest problem in life is a sense of inadequacy, a sense of finititude. I want to fly and reach the skies, but am unable to defy the law of gravity. I feel like walking on the surface of water, no way says gravity, you drown. The only concession I get is to lift my feet which enables me to walk or jump a few feet. The fastest of athletes takes almost ten seconds to cover a small distance of hundred meters. My mind travels much faster than that.

The air I breathe to keep myself alive, the food I consume, the water I drink come from mother nature. The five elements which constitute my body space, air, fire water and earth all come from nature and after the death of the body go back to their home.

This sense of finititude, this limitation is my problem, my bondage. Almost zero autonomy, total dependence on external nature. All our desires arise out of this sense of finititude and heteronomy. My ego the power of self assertion finds it difficult to admit and I continue to look for happiness in the objects, by possession. The potential perfect or infinite which summons me, but my limited mind thinks that completeness of being can be felt by clinging to the object. A new desire arises the moment one is fulfilled there is release of tension -a sense of satisfaction happiness but soon a realisation that I remain as incomplete or imperfect as before. So all pleasurable experience leave me asking for more, pleasure being temporary, lasting for a very short period and what ultimately follows is the pain. The more experience by way of perception of an object satisfies giving a feeling of fullness only to fall apart the next moment, because it is only an illusory fullness.

"So my dear wife' says Yagyavalkya nobody is dear. No object can be regarded as lovable or desirable.Neither the husband is dear to wife nor the wife is dear to husband. Neither the children are dear to father nor father to the children. All love, whether between husband and wife children, kith and kin, friend, wealth etc. is ultimately a reflections of love for the one's own self The whole idea of love for any object is fallacious you can never be immortal through mortal possessions or processes.

Strange though it may sound all love is love for the self. Maitreyi was really perplexed. The most loving husband, a sentiment which she has always reciprocated more than adequately was now being termed as a selfish attitude, a falsity. She had never thought of her relationship with her husband in a give and take manner. From her side, it was selfless love without any expectation of return all these years, and now suddenly this stigma of selfishness. Intelligent, as she was she well realized that the true contents were yet to come, the secret yet to be revealed.

The whole concept she was told has to be understood in the context of creation or cosmological descent.

It is the story of Adam and Eve having eaten the forbidden fruit and banished from the garden of Eden. Individual particularised humans banished from the kingdom of God, to the pain, tribulations and sufferings of the world. Death being viewed as the biggest enemy of life and life never-ending pain and distress.

In his discourse on immortality Yagyavalkya said to Maitreyi, 'Na pretya samjnasti' – After dissolution or death there is no awareness.

The whole idea is misconstrued by Maitreyi. She is totally perplexed. On one hand, the sage says that substantiality of everything, all knowledge is consciousness, while he says that on dissolution there is no consciousness, no awareness, and no knowledge. He then clarifies that our concept of knowledge is faulty. It is related to an object. It has to have content, without content there cannot be any knowledge. It is true in the empirical domain where subject is perceived or thought of as different from the object. In a work a day world this is different from that. However in the ultimate analysis truth is a singularity or non dual and this and that are the same. A total law of identity- eitad vaitad. Intruth, it is illusory because they are fundamentally the same. This is real knowledge- Knowledge by identity.

This is where western psychology and Indian Philosophy have different views. Western psychology can't appreciate the idea of consciousness without content. Perhaps Anna, since you have an elaborate background of western psychology you will be able to understand it better.

Anna admitted that in recent times the idea of consciousness has caught the attention of western psychologists. There is a clear distinction in the Pre-Freudian and Post-Freudian era.

If mind is symbolized by an iceberg, it was wholly conscious and floated on water, nothing below the surface before Freud. While his emphasis on libido, sexual nature of human desires and energy raised a controversy, but his modification of the iceberg, less controversial was path breaking. Now, one tenth of the iceberg was below the surface immersed in water, which contained ideas, feelings, memories which were considered forbidden and unacceptable and had been banished from consciousness to become the unconscious. Jung one time considered to be his heir apparent further modified the iceberg of which ninety percent was below the surface, concealed repressed as unconscious. But in all three icebergs consciousness was fully associated with mind, and Freudian psycho analysis in Jung had become analytical psychology.

I now frame a new model for the iceberg, said Rohit, which is based on the intuitive experiences of our sages. Here the entire iceberg being unconscious was drowned below the surface, mind being part of Prakriti – the matter principle, and consciousness representing an altogether different non-material principle – the Purusha of Sankhya philosophy. It was the Atma, undecaying, thereby immortal. Incidentally, all sexual urge was an urge for immortality by way of reproduction – Putra Eshna.

We now are confronted with a number of terms, body, Prana or vital energy, mind and consciousness or Atma. Atma becomes the fundamental postulate to which everything else becomes consequential.

A faint recognition of this concept got introduced into western psychology by the idea of transpersonal psychology. There is more to consciousness than mind itself, a discovery which goes back in time – a few thousand years back in India.

I think I'll narrate the Mandukya story and then we can discuss and analyse it. It is said that every dog has his day. Likewise every frog has his day, because Mandukya means frog. However, that was in a lighter vein, because this Upanishad was perhaps authored by a sage called Manduka, a strange name though meaning a frog. It can be termed as Bible of consciousness surpassing all psycho-analytical studies on consciousness.

It is the shortest of Upanishads with just twelve verses and less than two hundred words, has no stories, no symbols, no metaphor but such a deep significance that it has been stated that if it has been properly understood, then you have understood the entire truth of universe.

What is so special about it? It starts with an exposition of syllable Om –the sole, symbol used, in its three lettered form AUM. Aum is the Atma – the consciousness which is denotive of the perfect all inclusive Absolute-Brahman. There is no decay in consciousness like the body, so it is indestructible.

As long as it is outwardly oriented trying to grasp the gross objects, it acts in the operational mode of waking, along with all sensory perception.

This is what almost all of us except for a few psycho –analysts and yogis accept as the reality we sense every day.

Seeing is believing. Truth of the waking state which disappears once we are asleep. Body, mind both are active, with constant movement.

Next comes a mode where the consciousness is internally oriented, trying to get involved with relatively subtler object, a dream state. This is sub-conscious. Body is at rest and mind creates different scenarios, interpretation of which helped Dr. Freud to develop his theories. This is the state which has been called Taijasa.

A beggar can dream to be a king but a hearty meal in the dream world does not satisfy the hunger. It is more illusory and transient than the waking state. Here body is not active, but mind continues to be active, creating fanciful, dreadful, pleasant, unpleasant, all kind of scenarios for it's own pleasure. Paints a picture on your dreams from material embedded in the sub conscious and unconscious.

Now comes the third mode. Deep sleep undifferentiated homogeneity of consciousness or unconscious state.

While the objects of the waking world are perceptible, dream are products of our imagination. While actual water in the waking condition quenches your thirst, imaginary spring howsoever scenic in dream doesn't quench the thirst. We are either in a waking state, which disappears in our dream condition. The dream world crashes when we are awake. Yet we compare the two and feel that the waking world is more real. After all a dream is a dream. Who makes this comparison, one who has experienced both the states. We say that waking state has a practical utilitarian value. Actual food, actual water. A more rational, logical and impartial argument is that we carry our impressions of the waking state into the dream state and mind is not constrained by the social norms of morality and creates its own world including sexual fantasies. As Freud says that repressed sexual feelings can be liberated or according to Jung the general urge for growth and harmony between introvert and extrovert gets a free play and Adler says that our complexes are overcome. It's not God's world. It is my world and I create it according to my own proclivities.

However if we treat it as a carry forward from the waking state, then it becomes an effect of the waking state, the latter becoming the cause. We are now constrained to think whether our waking state is an effect of a cause which is more real than it. This is the philosophical quest in which the Upanishad engages us to search for the causal factor.

While Psycho-analysts of the west analyse it in terms of body and various states of consciousness of mind, the old sage-psycho-analyst goes beyond mind and identifies consciousness with Atma, or self, and after deep sleep enters into the transcendental domain which is the highest level subsuming all other states of consciousness.

The deep sleep is very relaxing, because there is no agitation either in the body or the mind, both of which are at rest. No dreams, no desires, no objects to disturb, blissful in a way. While mind is at rest, ego is absent, but there is a veil of ignorance as there is no awareness. This is the state of Prajna – cosmic counterpart is Ishwar, Lord who rules-the executive power of the Absolute.

The transcendental state Turiya is neither outwardly oriented nor inwards, nor a combination of internal subjective and external objective. It has no qualities, no attributes. Invisible, ineffable,incapable of being grasped by intellectual learning. Where all phenomenality is subsumed, auspicious, peaceful, non dual, quintessential unity of consciousness, the grand fourth is the Atma-pure consciousness in its pristine glory. Transcendental state of consciousness- indescribable in finite terms. It can only be experienced by way of self realisation.

What has the modern Indian Philosopher has to say about immortality and rebirth? We revert back to the revolutionary iconoclast philosopher Aurobindo.

Starting with Gita, the song divine dictum that a person discards his worn out garments and takes new ones, so does the immortal soul casts off its bodies and joins itself to others that are new. The immortal soul is unborn, ancient, and everlasting, it is not slain with the slaying of the body.

Birth then according to him is the first spiritual mystery of the physical universe, death is the second which gives its double point of perplexity to the mystery of birth. Life which otherwise would have been a self – evident fact of existence, becomes itself a mystery by virtue of these two which seem to be its beginning, and its end, are only the intermediate stages in an occult processus of life.

We are totally unaware of the 'unknown before' and 'unknown here after'. How do we proceed?

Science does not come to our rescue. It deals only within the empirical domain – Anything which can be verified in a laboratory. The whole idea is beyond observable facts. A blind alley so as to say.

Psychology rather than physical evidence has to be taken recourse to. Memory fades away with time and distance. That's a very poor aid.

The only way left with us is that beyond observable facts, we must be content with reasonable logical satisfaction, dominant probability and moral certitude – until we upgrade our sensory and intellectual capacity to a level where we exceed our normal perceptional and mental spectrum so we have accessibility into the unknown ultra – violet and infra red zone of consciousness.

King Janaka queried from Yagyavalkya as to where does one go after death? Do you fully understand as to where you are at present? You want to know about your future. Do you fully understand your present? Is everything about your life crystal clear? No invisible areas, no doubts? 'Well nobody understands life fully. When you are in your waking consciousness cannot understand your present fully, there are dark areas, grey areas then how can you know about the future. Your present is determined by your past and in turn present determines the future. This is the essence of the law of Karma. Once you fully understand the time process then past present and future merge into eternal present

Chapter - 23

NARAD

'Om Purnamadah Purnamidam, Purnat Purnamudachyate, Purnasya Purnamadaya, Purnameva Avashishyate'.

Purnahuti Hom mantra is a very significant Philosophic mathematical equation which also is the invocation prayer of the largest Upanishad – Brihadaranyaka – the Upanishad of the great forest. It is an equation which explains the idea of differentiation and integration both – the fundamental principles of calculus.

It is said that the two concepts of zero and infinity originated from India. Aryabhatta and Brahmagupta are credited with the idea of zero and the mythical serpent on which rested the sustainer god Vishnu was Ananta Shesh – one which had no beginning and no end an unfathomable expanse, endless cycle of creation and dissolution – involution and evolution.

It is one thing to use a concept for mathematical equations, but quite another to fully understand it. In India mathematics had a symbiotic relationship with philosophy and intertwined metaphysics. It originated with the Veda text. The auxiliary texts of Veda were known as Vedanga.

Vedanga Jyotisha or astrology was called Veda Chakshu – eye of the Veda. The fascinating movements of stars and planets led to astronomy and astrology and origin of Vedic mathematics. Mathematics as the head of all branches of learning was compared to the crest of the peacock and the crown jewel of the serpent. Rig-Veda spoke about suns wheels with twelve spokes revolving around the earth endlessly and the fire in it mounted the 360 couples containing 720 people, 360 nights and 360 days.

Now coming back to the equation, what does it say?

"That is full, this is full. Form the full taken out the full, yet what remains is the full. A paradox in mathematical terms but a profound philosophical statement."

Both zero which is 'Shunya' in Sanskrit denotes a void, a total absence of objectivity, so does the infinity where all objectivity is subsumed. Incomprehensible to the ordinary human mind. We cannot visualise either of the two.

Now let me start with Om or a unique word – a verse highly symbolic in its purport AUM, each syllable denoting some measure or quantum followed by an immeasurable or quantum less silence.

Let me revert back to the magnum opus or piece de resistance of Vedanta philosophy – Mandukya Upanishad. Text containing just 12 verses, 24 lines, about two pages and less than 200 words, the entire Vedanta philosophy compressed in these 12 mantras or verses, strange but true. 'Mandukyam ekam eva alam mumukshunam vimuktaye' – Mandukya Upanishad if properly understood alone is enough to solve all the mysteries of life.

A text where there are no characters no stories, no metaphors except for one great symbol literal figurative all in one which denotes the All inclusive Absolute or God. The commentaries and the glossaries are much more voluminous than the original text.

The sage philosopher psychologist got his wake up call from deep sleep and took the mystic syllable as the symbol for explaining various states of human consciousness. AUM became the Bija mantra or seed for every other mantra. The sage psychologist, in his psycho – philosophical analysis went on to investigate the concept of Atma or self, the four stages – transcendence, the lowest getting subsumed in the higher and laid the fundamental foundation of meditational technique or Yoga.

Before elaborating on it and concepts of meditation let me intersperse it with an interesting story from another Upanishad called Chandogya.

Narada Muni, as he was popularly known in mythological texts was a sage divinity; one of the psychic sons of creator Brahma, who was a travelling musician and storyteller and a messenger of sorts. He had been a gandharva or celestial musician in his previous birth and was cursed to be born on earth and was born as a son of a servant who serviced a group of saintly priests. The name signified that he was a devotee of Narayan, god who is a pacifist. He was forced to wander around the earth due to a curse by Daksha Prajapati – one of the creators. He was never confined to one place but always wandering around – a wandering mendicant.

He was supposed to be a very learned sage with loads of experience gathered wandering around in different realms yet he approached another wise one, Sanat Kumar and requested him to accept him as a disciple. Sanat Kumar wanted to know as to what all Narada knew before proceeding further. Narada's reply covered almost all the subjects. He claimed to be proficient in Vedic treatises, epics, mythological texts, grammar, mathematics, astrology, astronomy, logic, ethics and politics, physical science, music art and dance. Almost every science and every art I have studied, yet I am looking for happiness and peace. "All this knowledge which you have is of no consequence" said the master. There is a difference between a surface knowledge based on appearance and the real content within. The knowledge you possess is more by way of information. Mere information has a limited utility in life. Information to be converted into knowledge requires entry into the 'being' the real content of a thing, from externality of an object to the internality of it.

How do I go about it? Was the next question? Now begins a discourse on meditation – Vidya so as to say.

Namo passva – start by meditating on name of the object – the lowest level from which they begin the ascent. The first step is conceptual meditation. The object is meditated upon as absolute. During meditation there should not be anything external to the object. The object represents a totality.'Name is Brahman'. The name the outer limit of the reach of the mind. According to Indian occult tradition, name is the gross manifestation of speech – Vaikhari audible word expression. But higher than the gross expression is the subtle principle of speech – paravak. Speech is the causal principle for name which is the effect, cause being superior to effect, one starts meditating on cause in the second stage. Beyond the speech and higher than it comes the mind. From expression we move to mentation, higher than it comes mental resolve, the will or Sankalpa. This will is the force or power of self – assertion. Every individual object asserts itself, even a tiny particle like an electron. The world in its generality and particularity is rooted in will. Higher than the will comes the memory aspect of the four fold mind organ. Memory is where all learning is stored. Beyond memory is Dhyana or the superior faculty of concentration of mind. Ekagrata – single pointed thought where whole souled absorption of thought is on an object. Meditation does not end here. Vijnana – understanding comes higher in the hierarchy. Now a new element is introduced i.e. Balam or strength Mind and body have to function in a harmonized way adding to each others strength. It is the psychosomatic power, mind and body energizing each other. The realisation of the strength within dawns on you, further strength is added by the forces of nature. Moral observances and psycho physical hygiene make the psycho – physical framework strong enough to with stand all problems during transformation. Now comes Anna – food all things material to keep the life going, keep the body and mind together. All the matter including food, water, air we get from the nature so we have to harmonise our self with Mother Nature. Food is followed by water, Tej or fire and air and space. Space is the subtlest of the elements. All objects are located in space, all movement; all experience takes place in the space. So the contemplation has to be on unbounded space. Now higher than space comes Smara – power of self – consciousness. It is an interiorisation process where we start meditating from the external to the internal. Now comes Asha or Hope, the possibility of betterment, a self – transcendent existence. Prana – or the life principle is the next in hierarchy. Imbued with truth, thought and understanding and Shraddha or faith contemplation moves to nishtha or steadfastness. Now comes a very interesting statement. Nothing can succeed in meditation unless it is propelled by happiness. All evolution has at its base an urge to happiness. Happiness is at the back of everything, main motivating power. Now, comes a million dollar question where does happiness lie. Is it in the mind or is it in the object. Individually taken it is neither in the mind not the object because both are finite. Here infinity comes into play. Happiness is a result of sense of infinitude. Yo vai bhuma tat sukham. "Happiness is plenum. Its infinity, completeness, perfection, absolute", Bhuma has no English equivalent. It conveys an absolute both in quantitative and qualitative terms. All happiness is in the infinite.

Narada curious to know requests his teacher to explain the distinction between infinite and finite. The answer form Sanat Kumara says that "When one sees nothing except one's own self, where one hears nothing except one's own self, where one understands nothing but one's own self, that is Bhuma – the Absolute or infinite, and where one sees something outside oneself, where one hears something outside oneself, when one understands or thinks something outside oneself, that is the finite".

Since infinite contains everything so anything coming out of it continues to be part of it and does not in any way deplete it. That is the solution for the paradoxical equation. The power of the infinite, it is something non relative, so all equations are only symbolic, all inclusive because nothing comes out of it and nothing goes into it. There is no I no You. It is Aatma Swarajya, 'Emperorship of the self'.

Reverting back to Mandukya Upanishad it follows a direct approach, No stories, No characters.

Aum becomes a symbolic transcendental principle beyond space time continuum. Space and time are the dividing factors in terms of specific location and past present and future. Being in space time also leads to the sense of inadequacy or finitude to be overcome by physical or psychological sense of possession. That's why we look for pleasures in objects. All these pleasures are transient. We feel hungry then food is the first preference. One the stomach is full, the desire for food disappears only to be reappear again after a time gap. Desires create a tension. Any release of tension is pleasurable. It is a stress buster. That is why sexual intercourse leads to release of tension, a temporary fulfillment of a desire and providing a sense of pleasure. The Upanishad has a threefold classification of desire. Asti – Yearning for immortality or external existence. May I live forever, never to die. Bhati – the urge to knowledge, because knowledge grants us the power, solves the mysteries of the universe. Priya is the urge for happiness delight.

What exactly is Vedanta was your question. It is the quintessence of philosophy propagated by the Vedic texts. Vedic treatises mainly Rig – Veda in Purusha Sukta and Nasadiya Sukta – hymns of creation outline a theory of creation, along with various liturgical practices by way of propitiation of deities – nature gods to begin with. It gets further refined to a philosophical doctrine in the Upanishads – the later part of the Vedic literature. Then come various teachers like Acharya Shankar, Ramanuja, Vallabh, Madhva and Nimbarka who interpreted the philosophy according to their own intellectual proclivities. In Brahma Sutra, Acharya Badrayana tried to reconcile various apparent anomalies between different Upanishad because they were authored by different people. Gita finally emerged as a text which tried to present a harmonised picture of various schools of philosophy like Sankhya, Vedanta and Yoga in a much more pragmatic and utilitarian framework without compromising on its spiritual content. It propounded the idea of Dharma – a law of integration which binds multiplicity into a harmony.

Mandukya starts with the waking state in which we normally experience the world – the live experience. It is explained in terms of our consciousness which is always keen to interact and grasp the objects – externally oriented to the maximum.

This is what we call living our life. All that matters is the present seeking pleasure in all experiences – live life to the full. The senses get attracted and stimulated by what lies in front of us, visible audible tactile – a reality which we seem to understand well. This is the first or primary stage of consciousness called Vaishvanara – the cosmic person. The analogy to cosmic person or mind also brings out a differentiation between Jiva – the human and Virat – the world person. Jiva is Alpagya. Alp Shakti and ekdeshika, one endowed with limited knowledge limited strength or power and confined to a single location, whereas the cosmic person is omniscient omnipotent and all pervasive.

This is where Yoga gets introduced. Jiva with his handicaps can move forward in the direction of the cosmic person by giving up his desires emanating from Ahankar- or the power of self arrogation. This was the state of consciousness which the western psychologists in the Pre–Freudian era dealt with. But dreams fascinated Dr. Freud and outcome was the interpretation of that state as one of sub – conscious.

The Indian sage psychologist in Mandukya gave a twist to consciousness interpretations from external world to the internal world of dreams form gross objects, it was now about the subtler objects, creation of dream world by the dreamers mind when body and senses are at rest. Taijasa it was called.

Further more important than the dream world was the third stage of deep sleep. Deeper does it delve into the terms of depth psychology.

Dreams according to Freud were caused by sexual impulses, Adler because of inferiority complex and Jung said that it was because of urge for growth and harmony between extrovert and introvert in us. From Indian psychologists view point it is an opportunity to fulfill the desires.

Now comes the important third stage – Anandabhuk – blissful state of happiness while it lasts – the deep sleep. Mind and body are at total rest, the physiological operations carry on without causing any disturbance. Relationless where there is no interaction with any person or object, no possession, no acquisition of anything of value, no food, no sex, a quietitude of which there is no awareness – the stage called Pragya or consciousness. The happiness in the sense that you feel absolutely fresh and energised after a good nights sleep is by subsequent memory of it. We were in an unconscious state of sleep while we were enjoying the bliss. What a paradox? The blissful state is that of which are not conscious of in a simultaneous way. What element in our memory tells us that all the fatigue disappeared and we were in a happy state for those seven hours of sleep. Unconsciousness could not have caused subsequent consciousness, therefore the natural inference is while every faculty including mind body and intellect was at rest, the consciousness was present to recall the experience of happiness. The only unfortunate part was that we did not consciously enjoy it. Consciousness existed during deep sleep without any content of it. It was conscious of itself. I am what I am, in my pristine purity. Instead of terming it as those seven hours of happiness, I dismissed it with a statement that I had a nice rest for seven hours ready to be yoked to the harness. One did not incur any karmik liabilities because there was no mental movement.

This gave the clue to the sage – psychologists that it was possible to reach a sage of total happiness with sincere effort and at the same time to be conscious it. An eternal blissful state beyond dreams and deep sleep of supra consciousness. The transcendent Turiya where space time did not matter. Seventh verse of Mandukya describes it in totality – consciousness is neither externally oriented to interact with the objects, nor internalized to create dreams, nor is a combination of the two. It is not dense clouded consciousness of deep sleep. This indescribable, relationless, unthinkable, without any characteristics is the quintessential unity of self which exceeds the phenomenal world of experiences, auspicious, peaceful non-dual, Aatma – the ultimate pure consciousness with total awareness.

This realisation is the one which provides the capacity to move from strength to strength. This is what Narada was told when he was exhorted to concentrate on Bala or strength. This also answered the question as to where the happiness lies. It is not in the objects outside. It is within and all the objects become part of the self or the self gets extended from individual to the universal by the process of attitudinal change a movement form psycho physical to the spiritual domain. That is the reason why meditation has been termed as a spiritual activity calling for a different mind set along with a discipline at both physical mental and vital level –various stages of Yoga are preceding it.

It is in this background, that Patanjali's eight limbed Yoga starts making sense – the aspiration to attain the level of supra consciousness. Concentration and meditation is more of a relaxation than effort. Meditation according to Patanjali is the penultimate stage of Yoga followed by Samadhi or absorption in the Absolute where the form almost disappears, swarup shunyamiva – surviving as an iota of itself.

Meditation is the most powerful technique for spiritual evolution. We have to go back to the concept of creation where the absolute in his executive power termed God – a force of consciousness ideates in a manner that he becomes many out of one – fashions material out of the spiritual. So in the involution process the subtlest of consciousness gets denser and materialised into a grain of sand which may have a very rudimentary consciousness concealed, so it is taken as inconscient and insentient. While involution process is the downward movement form subtle to gross, evolution is the ascent form the gross to the subtlest.

Evolutionary scientist who ignored the involution part of the cycle of creation was logically right when he stated that the supreme intelligence can be there only at the end of evolution because it is a march from inconscient to supreme consciousness – Perfecto Perfectus. In any in between stage –God as the supreme intelligence becomes a delusion. But taking the recurrent cycles of creation as involution and evolution, and dissolution a very pertinent question arises as to why the creative power takes all the trouble of projecting a world and then dissolving it.

Perhaps Einstein the philosopher sums it best when he says "God plays dice". It is a sport which he indulges in.

Why are we here? We were never asked to exercise a choice for being born and then serving a life sentence bounded by the walls of space and time – always full of desires and dissipating energy for fulfillment of desires. All philosophy tries to address the fundamental question as to why these limitation in life – why thrown in a chaotic disharmony struggling all the time to keep our head over the surface of water.

The first step is the recognition of existence of spirit and matter. Then a reconciliation between the two by Yoga – a mutual comprehension which finally results in a final unification in cosmic consciousness. Sentence to life bondage also creates an urge for fulfillment and release and then to find out a path out of our transitional egoistic life where death and pain are the essential parts to an immortal blissful existence.

But that does not answer the question as to the rational of creation or this world existence. Divine – a painless existence all blissful we pine for consciously or unconsciously. It exists during deep sleep but unconsciously, but has to achieve in a conscious manner through Yoga. Reconciliation of the contradictious of the phenomenal word – a world of duality and opposites into a unity is the final goal of evolution. Our egoistic preoccupation is the limitation where only the externals can be visualized not what lies within. We do not have the capacity to go beyond appearances and the desire to scale the high walls of space time and go beyond it.

Philosopher have given different explanations as to why the Absolute ideated and willed a universe throwing various species in a chaotic situation struggling for existence, fighting with each other, killing each other for survival and hegemony. There is no compulsion on the Absolute to create. Aurbindo says that it is for delight. It is a sport which the God indulges in. When Vedantic theory of cosmic origin term the Absolute as existence consciousness bliss is beset with two contradictions as to emotional and sensational consciousness of pain and ethical problem of evil. While Buddha treats life as entirely painful, Aurobindo says that if normal life is viewed in a dispassionate manner and neutral way, and with an unemotional appreciation we shall find sum of pleasure of life exceeds pain. We classify pleasure when we are overjoyed and pain rest of the time including neutral moments. The whole depth psychology in India was triggered by the great psychological paradox – being unconscious of dense consciousness in deep sleep.

In his commentary on Mandukya Gaudpada introduces the concept of Asparsha Yoga, non – contact union. This is what the modern physicist call the quantum entanglement, the communication between two particles located at a distance from each other, what Einstein termed as a 'spooky action at a distance'. The Turiya or the transcendent stage stresses the idea of non – location in space which EPR paradox unsuccessfully tried to contradict, because it violated the fundamental premise of speed of light, yet it was confirmed by Bells experiment and propounded by Northhead as process philosophy. Physics cannot comprehend anything non-material or quantumless as being of any significance. Depth psychology in India in a transcendental state of consciousness deals with the idea of consciousness without content – Quantumless silence of AUM.

Chapter - 24

JANAKA

It has been said that anything concerning philosophy, life ethics and religion etc. is not there in the Epic Mahabharata cannot be found in any other scripture or text. It is supposed to be a 'Magnum opus', all inclusive comprehensive, much beyond its historic connotations. Oldenburg said what started as a simple epic narrative ended up as a monstrous chaos. Eight times the volume of Odyssey and Iliad put together.

This interesting story which fully explains the concept of 'Jivanmukta' or liberated in life yogi also comes from Mahabharat. It in the Vedantic tradition also lays down the fundamentals of 'Laya Yoga' or yoga of dissolution.

It is difficult to say as to who is the hero in this story, King Janaka of Videha or his teacher Ashtavakra.

Ashtavakra suffered from a curse which came from his father. The intelligent child in the womb of his mother Sujata, interrupted his father Kahod for wrong intonation in the recitation of Vedas. Father in his anger cursed the child in the mother's womb to be deformed at eight joints. Incidentally phonetics or right recitation of the mantras was an important limb of the Vedas.

The poor innocent child, was born with eight deformities in his body and that is why was called Ashtavakra.

His father Kahod was a poor Brahmin, living in penury went to the court of king Janaka to seek some royal patronage and thereby earn some money. He lost a debate with the court philosopher Vandin who as a punishment sent him to serve his father Varuna.

The child brilliant though, was teased by his fellow students for being deformed and without a father. On being told by his mother that the father had gone to Janaka's palace and never came back, decided to visit the palace to find out the whereabouts of his father.

The twelve year old was stopped at the gate initially but later managed an entry to the court. Everybody including Janaka laughed at him because of his body deformities. The boy reacted saying that he thought Janaka was an intelligent person. But unfortunately, he was disappointed as the king like others could not see anything beyond his bodily shape. A wise man also has Atma drishti, an ignorant has Charma Drishti cannot see beyond the skin. He in a scriptural debate defeated Vandin and rescued his father. Father ever obliged to him asked his son to take bath in river Samanga and after the bath all deformities removed, walked out a young handsome charming boy.

King Janaka, the epitome of epistemic curiosity was so impressed by the young boy that he decided to accept him as a teacher and requested him to show the pathway to knowledge, liberation and renunciation.

There followed a discourse with the teacher saying, 'As one thinks, so one becomes'. One who considers himself free is free indeed, and one who considers himself bound remains bound.

You are neither earth, nor water, nor fire, nor air, nor space. Self has to act as a witness to all these- the embodiment of pure consciousness. All the elements constituting the body, mind intellect etc. become irrelevant and self realization is only path, where detached from the body you abide in pure consciousness.

You, who has been bitten by the great black serpent of egoism " I am the doer", please drink the nector of faith, " I am not the doer" and be happy. Burn the forest of ignorance with the fire of certitude, cut asunder the rope of body consciousness with the sword of knowledge.

A statement very strange follows. 'You practice meditation' – that indeed is your bondage. The very thought that ' I am meditating means you have not reached a stage of thoughtlessness'. There continues how so ever small an agitation in the mind just take a step forward and enter into supreme silence.

'O Marvelous am I, Salutations to Myself, There is none so competent in this world as me, is holding the universe eternally without touching it with my body. I am the indestructible one.'

It is not an ego- propelled empty boast of a narcissist king, but words of a 'liberated in life' mystic, who has conquered the passions of the world. A yogi in true sense, who claims that in Me, the limitless ocean, the waves of individual selves, according to their nature rise, jostle about, play for a time and disappear.

However, the teacher a hard core Vedantic would not let him go scot free so easily. He accuses the king of passion for accumulation of wealth, attachment to the illusory world of sense, acting under the sway of lust and indulging in sex, running about like a wretched creature, yet claiming to be a self-realized Yogi.

Yogi King takes up his spirited defense and justifies his behavior. The self-realized person who knows the self as 'one without a second' does what comes to his mind and has no fears from any quarters.

'Infinite as space am I,' says the king and the phenomenal world is like space in a limited jar- this is 'true knowledge'. Space is all pervading, substantial which appears as limited in a jar. 'I am the shore less ocean profoundly tranquil and calm. Waves rise and subside and disappear. I am really Pure Consciousness and for me the world is like a magic show.

The teacher now convinced of the sincerity of the disciple says that while distaste for sense objects is freedom, indulgence is bondage. Such indeed is knowledge. Now do as you please. I have fully apprised you of positives and negatives, now it is for you to decide you future course. The idea of 'I am' takes you to bondage. The idea of "I am not' takes you to freedom. Happiness belongs to a person who appears to other like a 'master idler' finding it difficult and distressing to open and shut his eyes. It conveys an idea of total dispassion.

The 'Great Idler' is neither excited in the presence of a sexy young beautiful maiden, nor does he fear approaching death. It is perfect equanimity. There is neither compassion nor violence, neither humility nor pride, neither wonder nor agitation. No craving for objects, nor any aversion for it. Ashtavakra conveys the extreme view that this universe is just a mode of thinking and has no reality as such.

Is there any text in which this discourse finds place? Yes, While Shrimad Bhagwat Gita is a dialogue between Lord Krishna God head and Arjuna the human representative, this one is called Ashtavakra Gita. A dialogue is between die-hard Advaita Vedanti Ashtavakra and Jivanmukta yogi king Janaka. It reconciles life in this world carrying on your daily activities of ruling the kingdom yet not involved. It is a lesson that what deep dispassion or non-involvement and desire less action is you can be a yogi yet carry on with business of life as usual.

Incidentally the final word coming from Janaka says that 'Nothing indeed emanated from me', It has been interpreted in different ways, but is a statement conveying a 'doctrine of non-origination' – Ajatvada. The doctrine of creation is a fiction which needs to be created to explain all that we perceive as the universe, whereas it is a recurring cycle of involution and evolution.

Non- origination has been explained by compaing the world creation with a spider creating his web from material within, he does not need external matter. So the immanence of transcendental has often been explained as the 'othering' of the Absolute, or a projection like a film being projected on a screen, where the various characters appear to be live walking, talking, singing and dancing in the garden. The form world is a projection of the objective force of universal consciousness or the cosmic mind.

Whether the world or universe is a reality or just an appearance has led to various schools of Indian philosophy. But the idea of "De hypnotization' of the consciousness of physicality and individuality is first step for spiritual ascent. It is a constant expansion into subtler and broader states of consciousness by gradual sacrifice of individual ego.

Well Bhagwat Gita is all about the whole cosmos being portrayed as 'a restless field, where dynamic powers are arrayed in a battle as if to extirpate themselves for a nobler cause'.

Incidentally, Kings Janak's credentials as 'liberated in life' Yogi, were suspect in the eyes of the so called learned ones, the priestly class, brahmins of the times. With a sense of spiritual chauvinism and upmanship they were not willing to accept a king indulging in worldly affairs and managing his empire as a Yogi. In their opinion a person being a king and Yogi at the same time was paradoxical.

The king aware of this criticism decided to invite the learned ones for a party where the most delicious meal was served. Seated in a row when the guests were totally enamored of the aroma of the food and were about to savour the delicacies, one of them looked and found swords hanging over their head tied to hair. His exclamation made everyone look up and all the faces were pale with fear. The delicacies were forgotten and they within minutes finished their meal without any sense of taste and came back to the court to meet the king.

'Hope you enjoyed your meal' said the king. Was the food satisfactory and did it meet with your expectation. Sorely disappointed they remonstrated as to what kind of a game it was, which the king tried to play with them. Forgetting all about the food delicious they were concentrating on the hair that was holding the sword, the tenuous connection. Likewise, the king said that his mind was fixed on Brahman alone. All the material objects and comforts of the world become irrelevant once you concentrate on the 'Absolute'. They could now understand the concept of a Jivanmukta 'a liberated in life yogi', who performed the normal duties of life while mind was fixed on the 'Absolute'. A supra mental status is attained through meditation. Jivanmukta, who is free even without dissolution of the bodily life in a final samdhi.

Chapter - 25

LORD BUDDHA

Six centuries before Christ was born a great prince in India Siddhartha Gautama, heir to the shakya kingdom. It is said that his mother died seven days after his birth and he was brought up by the second wife of his father king Shuddhodhana. He married his cousin Yashodhara and had a son named Rahul. The young prince living in his make believe world in his palace had the first exposure to the world outside – the encounter with the realities of a mortal world, when he saw an aged person advanced in years with a bent back bowed down by the years, a sick person counting his days, a corpse being taken for cremation by his relatives weeping and crying and a wandering mendicant who had apparently cut off all relationships with the world.

It suddenly became a big bad world full of suffering. The sightings shook him to the core and he left home and family to become an ascetic to escape from the pain and meanness of life and illusions of the flesh. After great effort, when he was about to give up, totally frustrated came the enlightenment.

After leaving the comforts of the palace lived like an ascetic practicing bodily austerities like fasting, body mortifications of the severe type till one day he smelt death, fainted by fatigue and sheer starvation.

There was a change of track – from austerity of asceticism having failed to meditation.

Seated under the 'Bodhi Vraksha' the tree of wisdom he facing east meditated without wavering and one fine day, wisdom dawned on him he was christened Lord Buddha – the enlightened one.

In the context of age he lived in it was like in history of EuropeanPhilosophy the Pre –Kantian era. The dialectic battle between Hume and Berkeley had left a void which woke up Kant out of his dogmatic slumber.

So was the case of India in sixth century before Christ. The great philosophical tradition of Vedas had been vulgarized. There were multiplicity of gods as well as demons, both having immense power to bless and glorify if pleased, and curse and injure if angry.

The sacrificial ritual with its violent adjuncts shook the conscience of Buddha. Violence, strange rituals were being justified on the basis of divine sanction by super natural powers. Barbarism of superstition was ruling supreme.

Sattvic knowledge, sage prophets of soul, renunciates in the true sense with little interest in acquiring wealth – the truthful Brahmin had been replaced by the greedy priest who said that you make a sacrifice to god and grease my palms, you can be absolved of all your sins.

Bhagwatgita referred to Zeitgeist – the time spirit when the lord incarnates himself for setting the things right, whenever anarchy, chaos and disorder – Adharma or erroneous interpretation of natural law prevailed. Buddha was a product to answer the need of the times. He became the spokesman of the age delineating the golden middle path. Although denying the existence of God and spirit, yet relying on his spiritual experience, he professed the four noble truths along with the eight fold path. It starts with stark pessimism that life is all pain and suffering where death rules supreme. It was the transient phenomenal world with unending wants and desire and craving for gratification of senses, which caused it and yet he relying on logic, psychology and purity of thought, the neutrality of the universal laws of nature suggested the way out. Treating everything as a flux, a movement, impermanent he interpreted life as a continuing series of manifestations and extinctions. He is one with Heraclitus in his discourse on fire, the flame appearing unchanged is changing every moment. When Heraclitus claimed that the world is an eternally living fire, he was symbolizing the metaphysical principle of becoming.

The apparent identity of a form was the continuance of an ever changing identity. There are two extreme ends – 'Everything is' one extreme, 'Everything is not' is the other. The truth lies somewhere in the middle. There is no being and no void. As Aurobindo said, that truth cannot be captured in a single trenchant equation. It is somewhere between Haeckel – the overarching philosopher of matter, trying to solve the riddle of the universe and Acharya Shankar for whom all things material are a delusion.

Six years of ascetic experience made him realize that truth cannot be attained if you have no strength left. Perhaps that is where meditation creeped in as an eight fold path where everything had to be right – belief, aspiration, speech conduct, mode of livelihood, effort, mind set and rapture. It was the moral code, the ethical ideal. Right action had to be unselfish action. No river can ever clean the doer of evil. To the pure every month is a holy month. Be kind to all beings. No violence in thought, belief or deeds was what he preached. Never in this world does hatred cease by hatred – hatred ceases by love. Victory breeds hatred because one who has been conquered is unhappy. One who conquers himself is the greatest victor.

In a manner of speaking the seed of yoga had been sown by Buddha.

It germinated in two different forms Raja yoga or Royal Yoga of Patanjali in the Sankhya philosophical tradition and

Hatha yoga in the tantra tradition omitting certain tantric rituals which the proponents of Hatha yoga found out of place and impure.

Patanjali the mystic philosopher like Buddha was of the view that pursuit of pleasure in a phenomenal world is invocation of pain. Nescience or ignorance of truth along with ones consciousness of finitude leads to suffering and pain.

Nescience or Avidya, an ignorance of truth had been defined in just one line sutra. Transient appears to be permanent; pain appears as pleasure, non – self masquerades as self and impure is accepted as pure – a total inversion. That is how we infer that empirically we are bound and transcendentally free. What you have suffered in the past cannot be rectified but future can be brighter if we get rid of nescience by way of right knowledge. Satyam, Gyanam anantam Brahman, says shruti –Truth is knowledge of the infinite Absolute.

Vivekkhyati – the right knowledge whereby you can discriminate between the transient and permanent, truth and falsehood. Taking a cue from Buddha, Patanjali's Royal Yoga has primarily been about communion with God by way of meditation. Meditation being the pen – ultimate stage of yoga, following concentration, rest were the preliminaries necessary to make a person fit for meditation.

It would come to you as a surprise that Patanjali did not prescribe any postures for well being or meditation. Out of 196 Sutras, just one described Asana– the physical posture. Steady and the most comfortable posture should be adopted. Whether you meditate standing, sitting or lying down it's your choice. All the asanas are later development. No wonder, someone remarked that Patanjali's Yoga though a brand equity has no relevance in the modern era which follows a different genre –named Hatha yoga with emphasis on Asana and Pranayama – bodily postures and breath control.

Because of Buddha's popularity meditation became a buzzword for people of the era. Two practices which caught the imagination of his followers were 'Vipassana' and 'Anapansati', which in the modern jargon is often referred to as mindfulness.

After Buddha's death there arose various schools interpreting him in different manner. The Hinayana or the 'narrow path' and 'Mahayana' – the greater path, offshoot of the greater path were 'Sahajayana' or the spontaneous way and Vajrayana or the tantric tradition where indulgence in sex was an acceptable way to awaken consciousness.

The fundamental postulate of Tantrism was that nothing is evil in this world.

Chapter - 26

ACHARYA SHANKAR

The story of Indian philosophy and psychology would remain incomplete without Lord Buddha. Once we talk about Buddhism, Acharya Shankara willy-nilly finds a place in the story- a very strong protagonist of a doctrine of subtle thought, remorseless logic and austere intellectualism termed as Advaita Vedanta. A symphony of spiritual philosophy where the ras- essence, alankar- the ornamentation, saundarya- the aesthetics and laya- the rhythm combine in presenting a most cathartic and sublime version of Indian thought.

We with a certain parochial bias, have a claim on his thought because he had set up a monastic retreat at Badrinath and had his Mahanirvana his final journey to the other realm at Kedarnath.

He wa born in a village called Kalady in Kerala. His parents wcre great devotees of Lord Shiva. They named him Shankara which represented harmony and equanimity.

Shankara extraordinarily brilliant with a rare gift of soul and intuition was perhaps a born renunciate. He was very fond of his mother who would not consent to his becoming a renunciate.

However the story goes that he went for a bath in a river with his mother and called out to his mother saying that a crocodile had caught hold of his leg and was dragging him into deep waters, and requested her to give consent to enter into aapat sanyasa- emergency renunciation without any rituals. The mother in order to save her son agreed and he prayed to Lord Shiva. The crocodile went away and he survived as a sanyasi henceforth for rest of his life.

First systematic exponent of Advaita Vedanta Philosophy was Acharya Gaudpada author of Karika on Mandukya Upanishad. Gaudpada's disciple was Acharya Govindapada residing on the banks of river Narmada. Acharya Govindapada initiated Shankara into the holy order of Vedic sanyasa.

According to Paul Deussen all Indian philosophy after Shankara is a footnote to his Advaita Vedanta.

It is also said that once he was asked to introduce himself, he said that I am neither the body consisting of five elements nor the mind,I am pure blissful consciousness. The real auspicious one.

Taking leave of his guru after having spent four years with him,he travelled to various places and arrived at Varanasi. All this while he had been engaging in discussion with scholars of various schools of thought. In Varanasi he had a philosophical debate with a great scholar by the name of Mandan Misra. Mandan Misra finally conceded defeat and later became Acharya Shankara s disciple by the name of Sureshwar Acharya. Mandan Mishra s defeat was not very palatable to his wife Ubhay bharati who challenged Acharya Shankara. She asked him questions on sex and erotica. Shankara being a celibate pleaded ignorance. After having accepted defeat he asked for a months time to gain knowledge of sex and erotica. By yogic power his soul entered in to a dead body of a king and with his queen learnt the art of sexual love. He came back for the debate after a month but Ubhay bharati rechristened as Vidushi bharati accepted him as the greatest scholar.

The life history needs a few explanations. First the crocodile is a symbol of attachment to the worldly pleasures. Secondly renunciation leading to denial of life in the world, it's ups and downs leaves some kind of void in knowledge.

Diversity, plurality and social life is as Important as the concept of unity. Body mind and soul need to be harmonised - a philosophical amendment which was professed by Aurbindo- who said the truth has to be found on the middle lane between the denial of the materialist and refusal of the ascetic. A synthesis of life with the divine – Haeckel read with Acharya Shankara.

Within a supposedly small life span of thirty two years he replaced Vedic ritualism with the philosophy of Gyana-Knowledge of the supreme spirit.

Among his works which reflected best of his thought is his commentaries on Prasthan Trayi- the triad of Upanishad, Brahmasutra and Gita.

His greatest exposition has been of The Atma – the eternal spirit which cannot be apprehended by any book based knowledge or by logic. It is the fundamental premise and everything else is consequential to it. Nobody can deny his own self because it would imply a denial of his own existence and then denial has no base. No one thinks that I am not. Descartes said I think therefore I am where as Acharya Shankara said that I am therefore I think. Existence precedes all thought. The self is prior to the stream of consciousness.It is the fundamental postulate which is to be taken for granted- period.

He reiterated the Yagyavalkya formula of Shravan manan and Nidhiadhyasan. Sense, reflect and meditate on self.

The great philosophers are a product of their times, projected by the zeitgeist or the time spirit. When Hume. demolished Berkeley, Kant was woken out of his slumber and entered the scene as the Copernican philosopher. So was the case of Buddha whose mission it was to set aside empty philosophical speculation and heaven seeking rituals involving violence of animal sacrifice and restoration of humane consideration in the society.

His reformatory message was of love compassion ethics wisdom guiding people to a doctrine of enlightenment or freedom by being better human beings. It was when the seed of Advaita Vedanta was sown with emphasis on Yoga, practical ethics and removal of suffering. Buddha in course of time became the deity of the era catering to the needs of the people.

Various tones emerged from his teachings and in the interpretational conundrum emerged Kshanikvada- the doctrine of impermanence, and Anatmavad-doctrine of non self and finally denial of God.

God as a concept is a great necessity for the humans, as an entity whose shoulders are needed to cry upon, who can be blamed for being unjust and cruel yet whom you can look for succour in bad times for hand holding in the obstacle race that life is. The father figure performing multiple roles,benefactor punisher justice provider sustainer all in one

With God denial were emerging sectarian views based on bacchalanian and orgiastic doctrines of degenerate tantrism.

Here a Copernican philosopher like Kant was the need in eighth century AD in India, to end the chaos and restore order. The answer to the problem lay in Abhyudaya and Nishreyas- secular welfare in the empirical domain and spiritual felicity and freedom in the trans empirical. Acharya Shankar with hard core non dualism and Ramanuja with his doctrine of qualified non dualism were there to provide answers.

Chapter - 27

CHARVAK

Your initial purpose for visiting India was to have a deeper understanding of contemplative psychology as enunciated by the Indian masters, both old and new age.

In a philosophical context we start with the idea of Panchakosh- the five personality sheaths. The external outermost and grossest is the food sheath, totally material denoting the body consisting of flesh blood and muscle etc. Then comes somewhat subtler, the second sheath prana- the vital life force, again material in content. Thereafter we move to the psychological domain the mind sheath and intellectual sheath each subtler than the outer ones and finally the blissful sheath, subtlemost. The externality or internality is not physical or spatial. It is logical. The more internality makes it subtler and intricate. Contemplation is the process of internalisation of thought process, a mental exercise where we explore the hidden potential of our mind, testing it's capacity, the potential for upgradation.

Now I will narrate an interesting story of Bhrigu the sage, son of Varuna.

Bhrigu inquisitive about the ultimate truth approached his father Varuna and requested him to apprise him of reality of Brahman. Food, symbolic of matter is Brahman. The first sheath, the first gateway to Brahman. It starts with gross matter. Then you enter the inner circle, somewhat subtler, Prana is Brahman, the second sheath, the second gateway. The we move to yet subtler third sheath, mind the third gateway. Bhrigu had learnt a very important lesson. The significance of matter. From food all things are born, food sustains life and body and on dissolution elements of matter go back to their origin. Period. But Bhrigu knew it was only partial truth. He contemplated by performing Tapa or penance and went back to his father for further enquiry. Father advised him to perform penance and find the right answers. Prana or life was transient therefore it could not be the final solution. Now he contemplated on the third sheath. Mind the storehouse of knowledge, but found it inadequate, because mind had no self luminosity. It was after all an organ for cognition which was not autonomous. It depended on some other entity to perform it's function. Contemplating he moved inwards to the fourth sheath the knowledge gateway. Again, he was not fully satisfied, because knowledge though superior and subtler than mind had it's own limitations. It was finite so under his father's guidance he moves on to the fifth sheath, the blissfull one, Anandmaya. Here he encounters bliss and realises that it is the last gateway to his destination, bliss infinite, pure consciousness- existence consciousness and bliss infinite, a supreme unity. His father led him step by step. There was no jumping and overstepping. Each phase or stage had a significance of it's own.

He was asked to take a vow not to reject food. The importance of food or matter was extolled. Body, life, mind and intellect have as important role to play as intuitive wisdom in quest of truth. Contemplation, penance is the praxis.

The matter is the ultimate reality, body and life is there to be enjoyed to the hilt. There is only one life, no herein before and no afterlife. Some say it was the philosopher Brihaspati, while others say it was Charvaka the proponent of this hard core materialistic philosophy. It did not go beyond the first two sheaths. Charva was the chewer of self, and Charvaka, meant a sweet tongued glib talker.. Contract debt and drink clarified butter, there is only one life, live it with pleasure unlimited. Eat, drink, and be merry. There are no karmik assets nor any liabilities. It begins with birth and ends with death. No baggage from the past, and no residue for future. That perhaps may be the truth. This text was of Lokayats. All is confined to this world. Nothing beyond it. This is the only lok- the one and only plane of consciousness. Just do not worry about sin, virtue vice soul God etc.. The sense perception is the only reality and evidence. Believe what you see or hear. No scriptures, no second hand knowledge. No authority of religion or philosophy has any value. Only elements like earth water fire and air, have a value and wealth and enjoyment are the only objectives of life. There are only four elements and matter is the only reality from which arises consciousness as well as intelligence by some strange process of mixing. Brain starts secreting thought that intelligence as well consciousness disappear on death. There is no soul and body is the only reality. It is hedonism pure and simple, totally unqualified.

While life is yours, live joyously to the hilt No one can escape the clutches of death,

Once our frame the body is burnt and reduced to ashes, How shall it ever return again.

Pleasure unlimited, sensualism, self assertion bordering on selfishness became the key words, individual will the dominant force and ideas of compassion, virtue, merit and God were confined to scrap bin. It was all a play of nature to be accepted as such. There does not exist any heaven, salvation has no meaning, soul doesn't exist. The philosophy, the Charvak school perhaps was a very strong reaction to the degenerate form of religion where dogmatism along with superstition, sorcery, magic and exploitation of masses by the a pretentious priestly class had created an environment of revolt and reform. Since it challenged the prevalent rituals and ideas about heaven and hell and orthodox systems, it did not find it's true place in the philosophical hierarchy of India. Majority of us while paying lip service to spirituality, follow the material path. Some intellectuals going up to the fourth sheath. No wonder that some foreign interpreters were more favourably inclined towards this philosophy. It was " Logisch beweisende Nature klarung" – logically proving explanation of nature. Godless, no duty, no karma no rebirth, a simple doctrine of annihilation after death. It emphasised that there could be pleasure without pain. Is it not what we normally desire. A painless existence with as much pleasure as humanly possible. A philosophy good, bad or indifferent which by and large we follow with occasional hiccups. The tragedy with this view point was that it challenged the existing system and therefore termed heterodox and was pushed aside. Yavat jivet sukham jivet could be interpreted in two ways. Pursuit of pleasure irrespective of means for attaining it gave it a somewhat negative individual hedonistic connotation, while happiness for all, greatest good of everyone could be interpreted in the best traditions of utilitarianism. The primary concern was for maintaining a healthy body by begging borrowing became important because that was greatest asset which an individual possesed. Entire life depending upon the maintenance of a healthy vitalised energetic body. The first two sheaths were the fundamentals of an individual personality to be looked after with great care. Denial of soul, rebirth denoted a clear diversion from the vedic tradition. It was open challenge to the prevalent orthodox systems. Therefore there were hardly any texts interpreting it in an unbiased manner.

However another important reason for overlooking the philosophy of Lokayats is the intellectual domain in the human mind, which doesn't like to rest at a place.

A thinking person always thought that there has to be someone more powerful than us. More majestic, more perfect and mind manufactured deities, devatas. They were conceived as the shining ones without a gross body. A stream of forces, compassionate just, and virtuous.

Human personality has multiple facets. In it's instinctive mode we seek pleasure. Soon we realise that pleasure is limited by time. There is nothing like perennial pleasure and it is followed by pain which often is absence of pleasure. Thus hedonism and utilitarianism become fallible doctrines. The higher faculty of reason comes into play. We start distinguishing between pleasure and pain, good and evil, virtue and vice, and strive to combine pleasant with good, happiness with goodness. This is the beginning of Yoga, the science of life. Material prosperity and worldly pleasures also make you aware of existentialist suffering. Angst cannot be wished away. Most of us prefer living a life with transient pleasure and consequent suffering. Life with a sense of neutrality, accept things as they are with effort to tilt it towards pleasure and avoid pain to the extent possible. A normal life. However a person with epistemological curiosity- a philosopher, sage or saint starts going beyond the gates. They start thinking about previous lives, life and after life, rebirth, elevated states of consciousness. Yoga becomes a practice, an art, a science and philosophy for perfection by invoking the grace of God, a symbol of perfection.

From instinctive desire prompted action, a person moves aided by morality and reason towards desireless action or nishkama karma-karmayoga. Then intuitive wisdom takes a person to the transcendental plane of gyanyoga. Mind becomes overmind- the new sovereign replacing senses and mind.

For persons with an emotional bent of mind is a path in between-Bhakti yoga, the path of devotion.

Chapter - 28

FINAL TAKEAWAY

Aboard the Lufthansa flight to Munich Anna was reflecting about her Indian journey where she had come ostensibly to learn about elements of contemplative psychology as elaborated in Indian scriptures by sage philosophers, but the take away was contentwise much heavier than what initially she had bargained for. Here was a philosophy which was not circumscribed by the contents of mere empirical experience but went beyond that into the transcendental realms of truth and non stultified knowledge ever so full. The plenum of fullness, infinite which never depreciated. It was the comprehensive concept of spiritual self realisation expressed in an extraordinarily logical manner while taking recourse to the best which intellect and reason could offer.

Shravan, manan and nidhiadhyasan were not only the key words she learnt, it was the golden key where by with the instrument of a purified body mind and intellect you opened the door to intuitive wisdom, thereby discovering your Atma veiled all this while due to nescience or ignorance. Try to know thyself and you know everything. What a dictum?

However ashram dharma offered a unique window to lead a life catering to your practical needs. Not everyone has to aim for perfection and be God. Even a few baby steps Godwards made you a better person, virtuous, compassionate and more humane spreading the message of universal love. A wide choice was offered as there were no commandments. Yadiccha tada kuru. You have been exposed to all philosophies, orthodox heterodox, material, spiritual, worldly transcendental, accept what appeals to you the most. Many mantras were reverberating in her mind.

Out of thousands who aspire to be a yogi, a rare aspirant is able to walk the talk, and ultimately the rarest of the rare achieves success. It is near impossible to be God or even Godlike in a short span. That's why it has been compared to the arduous task of walking on a razors edge. Follow the path of yoga living in harmony with your own self, with the world around including your fellow beings and finally with God, the supreme Person unique, ubiquitous, indescribable to be approached through symbols and metaphors by way of rituals. Jap sadhana on an idea supreme could be one of the ways. It certainly makes you a better person, spreading peace, harmony and love all around and the best possible healer. You have to be like enlightened Arjuna, human as well as humane guided by Lord Krishna, the god principle, representing the divinity within. Practical utilitarian as close to the ideal as you can. Sarvabhuta hiterata. Committed to the welfare of everyone.

She was going back as a psycho therapist with a liberal mind, an expanded intellect, an ever guiding spirit and a kinder heart- an ideal combination. A strange blend of idealism and pragmatism fit to spread a message of a healthy body, mind and spirit.